SMUGGLER

Robert Stark
Smuggler

All rights reserved
Copyright © 2024 by Robert Stark

No part of this publication may be reproduced, distributed, or transmitted in any form or by any means, including photocopying, recording, or other electronic or mechanical methods, without the prior written permission of the publisher, except in the case of brief quotations embodied in critical reviews and certain other noncommercial uses permitted by copyright law.

Published by Spines
ISBN: 979-8-89383-377-5

SMUGGLER

A LIFE OF DANGEROUS ADVENTURE

ROBERT STARK

"My Life Story? You wouldn't believe it if I told you. Hell, I have trouble believing it, and I was there!"

FOREWORD

I have always believed that there are a great many things that parents teach their children—things that help them to understand others, know when someone is joking, help to know how to fit in, or even how to feel love. I began to believe this because, when I was in my teens, every day I would find myself clueless and full of questions about one interaction or another, while I would see others seemingly know without question where they stood. At first, I could not figure out how. I knew I was not dull; in fact, even people I felt were seemed to have this mysterious knowledge.

I eventually came to understand that the vast majority of people have a sense of self at least partially based upon their parents. It is so innate that they are completely unaware of it or the effect it has on their every waking moment, good or bad. If you tell a person that this is so, they invariably cannot understand what you are suggesting, so incorporated into their persona it is. They cannot separate themselves from this mental picture of themselves, it being a big part of what they use to define who they think they are.

Now you might ask what importance this revelation has to the story that follows. Its importance is in helping the reader to understand the why of many of the actions and experiences I will relate here. If you find the events and experiences I chronicle here hard to believe, I completely understand. I sometimes find them hard to believe myself, and I was there. All names have been changed to protect the guilty!

CHAPTER 1

NEW MEXICO

I will not bore you with endless childhood memories; I have few anyway. I was born in the 1950s in a small town in New Mexico, or at least that is what is on my Birth Certificate. My parents' real home was Los Alamos National Laboratory. As at that time, this was a Top Secret base where the atom bomb was invented and where the most sensitive weapons research was ongoing. Understandably, this place "did not exist" for security purposes. My parents were two of the hundreds, if not thousands, of civilian scientists working with the highest clearance on the most cutting-edge weapons research at that time.

Their work, as you can imagine, exposed them to many dangerous elements, not the least of which being various radioactive isotopes. I have no idea why they split up, but my father left when I was 5. When I was 7, my mother told me my father had died. She was working at the Lawrence Livermore Radiation Lab by that time, and we were living in Livermore. I did not know it then, but my mother was also very ill. Cancer would take her life a year or two later. They were both in their mid-40s.

I remember running wild with my brothers with little guidance or attention from my mother. This, I came to realize later, was likely due to her ill health. I don't remember any loving or tender interaction with my mother or anyone else for that matter. In fact, as far as I can remember, I was never held or kissed as a child. I did get regular attention from my mother in the form of severe beatings. I don't think I was a bad child; quite the contrary. She was just overwhelmed by three very rambunctious boys, her job, and her advancing illness. By the time we moved to Berkeley, California, so she could work at the UCB/Radiation Lab, my persona had changed from happy to very serious. I consider this to be the end of my childhood. From this point on, I was paying attention, trying to figure the world out. I was an adult.

My mother died when I was either eight or nine; I can't remember. We had rarely celebrated birthdays or anything else, so I have no frame of reference. I do remember being called into the school office to be told my mother had died. They told me I didn't have to stay at school, so I walked home for reasons unknown to me. I wasn't worried about where I would go. I guess I was indifferent, having had little interaction with her save discipline.

I was sent for a time to live with some relatives back east who I had never met. First in Brooklyn, and then in New Jersey. I think they meant well and tried, but had no experience with a boy like me. In a short time, I was escorted back to San Francisco to be placed in a Group home (read orphanage). Except for a brief trip back east to be Bar Mitzvah'd, I never heard from or saw them again. I believe by this time I was already exhibiting symptoms of PTSD.

Left to fend for myself with no one to trust or ask questions of, I kept all my belongings in a knapsack ready to leave at a moment's notice. Of course, there were house parents and social workers, some of whom really did care. This, however, did not prevent them from moving me from house to house until I was the youngest in the house or the oldest. Not sure why but must have had something to do with my regular sessions with the social workers or psychiatrist. I came to the conclusion that none of the adults had answers to my questions, so were giving me their best guess which, of course, is all any of us can do. I realized I would have to figure out everything for myself. I did make one decision which I believe served me well for the rest of my life. I decided that to dwell on a past that I could not change was a downward path that if followed would quickly become impossible to return from. I decided that no one did this to me, it was just life and like it or not I must deal with it.

I was determined to live the life that I thought kids with parents did. I joined the swim team in high school and was 3 years all city. I then played water polo in my brief stint at college all despite being the only one with no family in the bleachers cheering them on. I took shop classes, built a sailboat in woodshop, learned the lost cast method in jewelry class, taught myself to scuba dive, how to work on cars, how to sail, and took Philosophy. These things and more I did on my own, self-motivating, including continuing to work out regularly which I have kept up to this day. I went through my life determined to expect the highest standard of myself working out and eating the healthiest foods. Even teaching myself how to cook so I could control what I ate.

At some point, I was no longer trying to equal others but was instead seeing how much I was capable of. This may be where my habit of trying harder and taking on increasingly difficult projects started.

Continuing to try to learn what I didn't know, figure out how I fit in, I needed to somehow acquire a sense of who I was, like everyone else seemed to have. It's funny but despite being rejected and passed along so many times, I always had a belief that if I put my mind to anything, I could understand it. Not sure why. As I internalized my search, going over and over every interaction attempting to understand the rules, I learned that I could visualize, design, and test in 3D. I could even run two parallel storylines, comparing them, to understand the possible outcomes well into the future.

I explored all the various "paths to enlightenment" of the time, deciding very quickly of each that they had no special insight so were of no value. I remember once in a high school philosophy class, the professor was explaining the good that would come from being introspective and facing your own fears. He looked at me as the class let out, then said I had such a calm knowing expression. He asked me if I was OK. I lied, told him I was, even though I was hopelessly lost, believing I would never figure it out because there were so many variables. By this time, I would sit for hours in my own world running possible storylines trying to learn the outcome of each. I was lost in thought most of the time until finally I decided I had to get to living, no matter the hurt. I went out to deal with the world. One of the motivating factors was loneliness. Another was my approaching the age when I would be booted out of the orphanage. I felt no amount of rejection or hurtful words could be worse than being alone with no chance at happiness. At least if I tried, there was a chance.

Still, I was walking around shoulders slumped, head down, with a crippling insecurity when dealing with others because I had no value, no one wanted me. Deciding I could not live like this, I set out to decide what attributes defined the kind of person I wanted to believe I was. Then I adopted those traits as my own to begin living as that person. This gave me a framework to reference when deciding what was acceptable or not. When asked to help a friend, even when that help would put me in jeopardy, or when pressured to betray a friend to save myself, it was immediately clear to me that if I did not help that friend in a time of need or if I sold out a friend to "save myself," I would instead lose myself. I would cease to be the person I wanted to be. I would lose being the person I was working so hard to become.

One of the first tests of my new persona came soon after. I had worked hard and saved enough to buy myself a little English sports car, an MG. One night while hanging out at the Daily City A&W, a friend of mine drives up in a brand new Triumph TR6 which was the competitor to my car. He had just 30 minutes earlier stolen this car and suggested we see which one performed better. We drove south on winding roads, racing until around 3 am when we found ourselves on the freeway at the Pacifica exit. I was in front. Not wanting to travel farther South, I took that exit. He followed, so we raced through Pacifica, looking for a way to get back on the freeway North. We passed a 7 Eleven with two police cruisers in the parking lot. I was a ways out front and saw them in time to slow, but apparently my friend behind me driving the stolen TR6 did not. On a straightaway, he flashed his headlights, so I pulled over. He pulled up behind, ran to my car, jumped in, and said, "GO, GO, GO." I looked in my mirror to see a police cruiser with lights on turning onto the straightaway. I managed to ditch them after a few turns but realized there were only two freeway on-ramps in Pacifica so we were probably trapped. I parked my car, and we took off on foot.

After a couple blocks, the police pulled up next to us and asked what we were doing and how we got there. I answered, "walking on the beach," and that we drove in my car. They put us in the back seat to have me show them where my car was. One officer got out, felt my tires, then said, "Yup, this is the car; tires are hot" (hardly admissible evidence). We were taken into custody then to the station where we were placed in separate rooms. One officer came into mine to begin questioning me. I refused to answer any question, knowing that my car was legal, so they had nothing on me. The officer said my friend was telling all and throwing me under the bus for Grand Theft Auto. He said he knew I didn't steal the

Triumph because I had my own car but would charge me unless I testified against my friend.

I had no intention of cooperating, even if he was telling all. Besides, I felt that their case was weak. I knew they always tell you your friend is ratting you out in a ploy to get you to talk. So I declined the offer. As it turned out, this time my friend was, in fact, throwing me under the bus. However, because they had only his testimony with no corroborative evidence, they were not able to charge me (nice tidbit of information I would use in the future). They had also found a camera that my friend stole from the Triumph then carried to my car, so charged me with receiving stolen property. I was told this charge would be dropped if I testified. I was not willing to give up my newfound ideals so declined this offer as well. I was assigned a public defender who should have been able to get such a flimsy case dropped with ease. Instead, through his inattention (read incompetence), I was convicted of the misdemeanor. This experience would affect some of my future decisions. The friend would go on to become a San Francisco police officer, which he could not have done with a Grand Theft Auto conviction. I never did get a thank you from him.

Years later, this same guy was busted in a corruption case within the SFPD. It seems some officers were looking the other way, sharing info with some of the Chinese gangs in Chinatown. Two of these gangs had been started in my high school while I, along with this former friend, were in attendance. He, being of Chinese descent, was friends with a couple of the guys who started one of the gangs. I always wondered if he wasn't an unknown member before he became a cop.

By the time I was in high school, I pretty much had the orphanage wired. There was an internal school for those housed there because most were too disruptive to go to public school. I, however, attended public school where I received good grades so was given some latitude. I was allowed to have a dog, plus I had a private room. When I took wood shop, I didn't want to make the standard first project, a box, so was allowed to build an El Toro racing sailboat. I joined the swim team thinking I wanted to experience everything I would if I had parents. Instead, it served to focus on the isolation and loneliness of being an orphan. I was a decent swimmer, being All-City for three years. The problem was that at the swim meets, everyone's parents, sisters, and brothers would cheer for them while I would get out of the pool to a deafening silence, even though I had won. The medals I received only reminded me, so I gave them to a girlfriend's daughter years later. I was even allowed to travel to Mexico a number of times with my Marine Biology Professor. He had finagled the loan of an official California University System van then had convinced Shell Oil to provide an underwater camera, film plus cash for food etc. We would drive down to Guaymas on the Sea of Cortes for Christmas and Easter with a select group of his students to study the flora/fauna of the area. In reality, we would camp to party with the all-girl group of chosen students until the last few days when I would jump in the water to take some films. Shell Oil would put these in their commercials trying to convince the public they were not polluting the environment.

Later on, I would find out one reason the people running the home might have been so accommodating with me. When I was 14, my social worker gave me an IQ test. This was a requirement, I was told, for any child in an agency accepting public funds. After taking the test, I was called in again to take another IQ test. I thought I must have screwed up the first. It was not until I was older, when I broke into the house parents' apartment to read my file, that I discovered I had scored comparatively high.

I should mention again that the people who worked at the orphanage were, for the most part, good people with good intentions. They had to be to put up with the abuse that I, with the other kids, heaped upon them. Some because they were angry, me because I didn't trust them. I call it an orphanage, but I was the only true orphan there (until my little brother was put in another house). The other kids were wards of the court, having been taken away from their parents. As such, every weekend and on holidays, they all would go home. I would be left there alone.

CHAPTER 2

I WAS A TEENAGE PUKA BARON

At 17.5 years, 1 moved out of what had been the only home I had known through my teens. I tried to follow the path that I had been told was the next step. I enrolled at CSU/SF as a Marine Biology major with a Pre-Med minor. I received SSI benefits from my parents so long as I carried a full load in school. To keep a roof over my head, I took a job as a lifeguard at night. To keep from starving, I would go down to Pigeon Point near Half Moon Bay, climb down the cliffs to a secret dive spot, then free dive for Abalone. At that time, you were allowed 7 per day. I had an old wetsuit (no hood or gloves), an old weight belt with an Ab iron made from the leaf spring off a car. I would climb down, jump into freezing water to get my limit most times by feel due to poor visibility. Then I would struggle back to shore with over 30 extra pounds of dead weight (no raft) to climb back up the cliff. Abalone is tasty but very rich. You couldn't eat it too often without having a coronary, so I would take them down to Chinatown. There, I would trade to restaurants for food. Abalone was not legally available at that time (farmed now), so they would feed me for a week for a couple good size ones. The downside was I had to eat in the kitchen so I wouldn't occupy a table. If you ever saw the inside of those kitchens, you would swear off Chinese food forever. Nevertheless, I did fairly well for a time, but eventually with no support plus no study skills, it became too much. Also, I didn't want to be a doctor. I loved the ocean but found Marine Biologists were paid so little they had to eat their subjects or starve. I dropped out of school. Now I needed to survive with no support, little education, or skills. I worked every angle I could picking up laborer jobs at construction sites (later carpenter jobs), then eventually making jewelry to sell on Fisherman's Wharf to tourists. Made good money until the city implemented a lottery for the limited spaces because of constant disputes. I put in but did not win, so with a friend Marcus (who was Mexican) I met on the wharf, I went to Mexico to begin importing. We would bring back Macrame' pot hangers, then special women's huaraches (woven leather sandals) that we had had made with wooden high heels. Sold great to the nurses at the medical center... Until they all had a pair!

Marcus and I then decided to go to the Philippines to try to source these new shells that surfers in Hawaii would string up for tourist girls. I had heard that some guys were buying them there so I sold my MG sportscar then borrowed $1500 from the Hebrew Free Loan Assoc. This Assoc. was created to help Jewish kids go to college. They only loaned if you stayed in school. The loan committee was made up of old very conservative Jewish Businessmen. I requested an interview after being turned down. An hour and a half of grilling later they reversed their position, broke their rules, then loaned me the money. Said I was a natural born businessman. An opinion I have proven incorrect many times since. I paid the loan off early.

Marcus and I set up a factory in Cebu with him remaining to oversee production. I returned to the United States to handle importation, sales etc. By Factory I mean a Quonset hut on the beach with a dozen women stringing shells. The Puka Shell fad lasted for a while (and has returned periodically since). We made good money but eventually the fad began to fade. Plus, I had to bribe Marcus out of a Philippine prison when he was accused of deflowering one of Dictator Marcos's nieces. It was standard procedure for President Marcos to take over any business that made money and there was no arguing. I also knew Marcus was fully capable of committing such an offense, so I didn't.

Now again, as would happen a number of times throughout my life, I found myself scrambling to remake myself. I needed to create yet another career persona. I was around 20 years old.

I tried importing everything from Italian red coral to semi-precious bead strands from Taiwan, to woven silver bracelets & belts from India. I went down to New Mexico to pick up Native American Silver and Turquoise jewelry which was popular at the time. With each of these, I found the margins too close for me to compete with the more established importers and dealers.

In casting around for a new direction, I looked

up some of the other guys I had been in the orphanage with. They were into drugs before and now were dealing successfully. Kevin was a fellow former orphanage inmate who was selling weed. I had no market to sell anything and no supplier but convinced him to partner with me. I proposed he would continue the weed business with me handling the emerging cocaine market. We rented a house in Mill Valley where I proceeded to look for suppliers.

I approached a friend, George, who I had met while in the wholesale jewelry business. I knew he had been in the drug business before so I reasoned he might know people who still were. He introduced me to another jewelry business owner, Al, who had connections so I was in business. My first large purchase, a kilo of cocaine, was almost my last. We were to do the deal at Al's place of business, a jewelry store, after hours. I was, as usual, punctual but his source was late. Unbeknownst to Al, there was a silent alarm that went on automatically at a certain time which was wired directly to the police department.

Al's source presented the coke. I sat with my back to the door weighing it on a balance beam scale. Suddenly the police burst in guns drawn yelling to keep our hands in view. Without hesitation, I stood up while at the same time scooping the kilo off the scale into my pants. I raised my hands then froze while Al convinced the police that it was his business. After they left, I had to strip to recover the coke which had spilled down my pants numbing my privates. So far so good.

CHAPTER 3

SOLO

The end to my partnership with Kevin came abruptly one day, after not too long, when he and I were driving to show a hashish sample to his weed contact. I was along for backup and because I had a car, a classic Mercedes coupe. It was the middle of the day, in the middle of the week. Suddenly, I noticed a police cruiser pull in behind me while an obviously undercover car pulled in front. The marked car behind then turned on his lights.

I pulled over. One of the officers approached my side of the car. He asked for ID and registration, which I produced. He asked if he could search my car. Before I could refuse, Kevin gave them permission. I had told them I was a jewelry salesman to explain our trip in the middle of the day. The officer then said that there had been a robbery of a jewelry store. He added we with our car fit the description. I took this as a laughably obvious attempt to explain an otherwise illegal stop, which I believe to this day was based on profiling. I was aware that if this ever got to court, such an obvious lie would not constitute "probable cause" any more than a passenger giving permission to search a car which he didn't own would. Not wishing to escalate needlessly, I got out of the car to watch as he opened the trunk. I had, as a matter of standard practice, placed the hash sample in a locked bank bag of the type used for night deposits. When the officer found this, he picked it up and asked me to open it. I replied that it was for deposit only and only the bank had a key (not true, but I felt he would not know the normal procedure). He squeezed and commented it didn't feel like cash. I just shrugged. Finally, on very shaky ground, having made up a story to allow him to pull us over without any probable cause, he returned it and let us go.

After showing the sample, Kevin and I headed home. It was now late afternoon on a clear day. As we approached downtown Sebastopol, we came up behind an older American car going very slow and weaving. I immediately noticed the three guys inside were wearing patched motorcycle club vests, so drove patiently behind them until they finally turned. At this point, Kevin popped up through the open sunroof and flipped them off. They saw this, so began chasing us. As they were a number of cars back on a two-lane road, there was not much they could do until we came into Sebastopol. When we stopped at a red light, a couple of the guys jumped out of their car and ran up to ours. We locked our doors. They tried but were unable to kick through the Mercedes considerable sheet metal. They did, however, succeed in breaking the taillights. The light changed, and I roared off, thinking, "This is broad daylight, where are the cops that pulled us over?"

After a mile or so, with no sign of them in my rearview mirror, I pulled over at a wide spot in the road to check my taillights. I left the car running and walked to the rear when suddenly they pulled up, skidding to a stop in front of us to the right. I jumped back into my car. By then, one of them had run in front of the car. He pointed a gun, ordering me to turn off the engine. I, of course, floored it! He fired, missing me by inches, putting a hole through the windshield before the car hit him.

His face impacted the Mercedes hood, then he slid up the windshield, taking out the wipers, to fall into the open sunroof. I continued accelerating back onto the road towards the interstate. I put my hand under him and shoved him back out the sunroof. I don't know what kind of drugs this guy was on, but despite serious injuries, lost teeth, blood streaming from his face, he held onto the sunroof and amazingly the gun as well.

The sunroof was electric, so it would not close with the drag of a human hanging onto it at 80+ mph. I am weaving around cars with his friends on my tail. Now the guy is trying to crawl into the sunroof. I should have stomped on the brakes and catapulted him, but it didn't occur to me, mainly because all Kevin had to do was release the guy's hands so he would slide off. Unfortunately, when I looked, Kevin was on his back kicking upwards, screaming like a child.

In trying to drive at approaching 100 mph, I was unable to battle him with one hand. He eventually got back in the sunroof, pointed the gun at me, then ordered me to pull over. With the highway looming ahead, and believing he would shoot, I pulled to the shoulder. Before the car came to a complete stop, Kevin jumped out to begin running around the front of the car. The bloodied but conscious guy, now sitting on my armrest, popped up out of the sunroof, yelled something, then went to shoot Kevin. I elbowed him in the groin; he fired and missed. Kevin, rather than helping me throw this guy out, continued across the opposing lanes of traffic, flagged down a car going in the opposite direction, got in, and left.

I don't know how long it took, but the guy on the armrest began kicking me in the face. Then, before I could react, his friends were dragging me out of the car. They held my arms while one kicked me in the ribs. The armrest guy again popped up out of the sunroof, saying, "Hold him, I'm going to shoot him." I twisted my right arm free and popped this guy hard enough that he fell backward out of the sunroof. I twisted my left arm free and took off across the freeway, expecting to be shot any minute. It was not until I reached and dove over a 6' chain-link fence on the other side that I finally looked back. They had not followed me but instead were dragging their friend to their car. They shot out my tires, tossed my keys into the field, then left.

After what seemed a long time, the police showed up. You would think they would have sooner, having been told of a high-speed chase with a guy on the roof with gunfire. All I can say is this was before cell phones. The police took me to the hospital for my broken jaw and ribs, then to the station. They told me they knew the guys and one was in the hospital, pretty broken up. I said I would testify against them, but one of the detectives said, "No, you won't." He went on to inform me these guys were suspected of a number of murders as part of a dangerous gang, so if I filed charges, I would never make it to trial.

The Detective told me this adding that I was lucky to be alive. He went on to say I was the first person he knew of to ever fight his way out with these guys. From that point on, they treated me with great respect. Then they asked me Kevin's name because there was a person calling in to ask if anyone was killed on the freeway today. They brought him to the station, treating him with noticeably less respect. The fucker left me to die in a situation he caused, after all.

The Detective was so serious when he told me about these guys that when I got home, I immediately packed to move since that address was on the police report. When I got the car back, I got it in running order then took it to an auto dealership in San Rafael next to the freeway called John Irish Jeep. There I traded the Mercedes for a used Honda. The salesman must have thought he made the deal of the century. They polished the car up, replaced the windshield, and put it up for sale on a raised platform visible from the freeway. A day after they put it up there, I got a call from the salesman asking if there was something he should know about that car. Apparently, someone tried to torch it the night before.

After breaking off my partnership, I continued doing business. A couple of older smugglers, who I had met through Kevin, contacted me, preferring to work with me because they appreciated my dependable and punctual style. I knew that the best way to get ahead was to be a source, with the best source being the guy who brought it in. I began to look for a way to do this myself. This group of older smugglers was a wealth of information which I soaked up at every opportunity. Importing was the most dangerous part of the business as it required making connections in usually third world countries where life was cheap. Then, once connected, one must arrive with large amounts of cash, very sketchy.

I continued dealing coke that I was getting, by this time partially from Bennie, one of the older smugglers. I had always limited my indulgence in my product, wanting to stay clear thinking, so able to avoid risks. Bennie did not limit himself in this way. Consequently, he was becoming increasingly difficult to deal with. One day I get a call from him asking that I drive him to San Francisco to see his attorney. I pick him up and drive to Union St. where the Law Offices are located. Out front is parked his lawyer's Rolls Royce Corniche convertible. Bennie jumps onto the hood, unzips his fly, then proceeds to urinate into the driver's seat while yelling out the lawyer's name. All the while, I am frantically trying to get him to come down before we get arrested.

I found out later that this attorney had taken a large sum of Bennie's illegal profits, promising to launder them to legal usable cash. I guess the attorney, instead of laundering, was living large on Bennie's money, returning none of it. Finally, I get him back into my car and back to his house. A week later, owing him half a million dollars but not being able to get him on the phone, I drove to the house he had rented for use on this coast. When I arrived, the windows were covered with plywood. I found him up in a tree with a shotgun, saying they were coming to get him. I contacted his wife and the other older smugglers who quickly collected him. Being high did not go well with the pressures of operating an illegal business.

My first actual smuggle besides a little weed from Mexico happened without warning. John, one of the older smugglers, being aware that I had experience with customs (from Puka Shells), came to me with a problem. It seemed that his group had a container from Thailand sitting down at customs that had arrived with none of the required documents. Also, they believed it was hot (suspect). I was asked if I could help. I devised a plan I thought had a chance of success, having gone over all the possible wrinkles in my head. I then looked up Harry, a friend who was a customs broker (and who had quite a cocaine habit). We steamed the Thai stamps from an old waybill and fabricated the missing bills of lading, waybills, etc., so that he could enter the container for delivery. I was sure that if this container was under surveillance, it would be released as a "Controlled Delivery." This was the term

Customs used for an operation where they would allow shipments to be delivered under their surveillance, knowing that the person who accepted delivery was just a paid worker, not the smuggler they wanted. They would then wait for the product to be delivered or picked up by the persons who owned it so they could bust them. I have heard that customs no longer does controlled deliveries with the actual product still in the container. Not sure if this case had anything to do with that.

To successfully pull this off, I would need to divert the Customs Agents' attention while, at the same time, spiriting away from under their noses a shipping container full of Thai Sticks. I sought out a self-storage facility that was made of screwed-together corrugated panels (they were common at this time). I rented two units back to back under different fake names. In the rear one, I parked a purchased van that was not traceable to us. I then unscrewed the panels separating the two units, leaving only a few screws to keep the panels from falling. Next, I called Harry to schedule the shipment for delivery. I had a friend, Jack, who I paid well, accept delivery, placing the container inside the unit with a rented forklift. He then, as instructed, locked up the unit and left to get lunch. While he was gone, we moved all the Thai Stick from the container to the van and re-screwed the panels. On schedule, Jack returned carrying a duffel bag in which were many more duffel bags with newspapers. He then spent some time crumpling the newspaper and stuffing the bags so they would look full. He added bags of sand that we had left for him to each bag for weight. Once ready, Jack began exiting the locker to load them into his truck. When full, he locked up the unit and drove to leave. At the street, Jack took a right. In short order, a parade of unmarked cars followed. We then drove the van to the exit, but we turned left.

I will not bore you with the details of Jack driving until finally being pulled over, except to say that he held his water. They could not prove he had any knowledge of the contents of the container, so they released him.

This was a one-time thing but did give me the sense that it could be done. It also earned me a new nickname...

CHAPTER 4

"THE KID"

Over the next few years, my business expanded. I gained a reputation as a serious guy who got things done, was careful, and trustworthy. I figured if I was going to do this, I should be a disciplined professional, especially considering the significant penalties involved.

I had experience with the police many times in my younger years. I was in and out of Juvenile Hall while in the orphanage for stealing cars, breaking into the school, or nothing at all, simply because the house parents wanted the house to themselves for the weekend (all the other kids had families who came and picked them up every weekend and holidays). I had a good healthy disrespect for authority, having experienced its arbitrary administration firsthand.

When I was still in the Home, I thought nothing of stealing a car (usually a Jaguar, big back seat) to go on a date, lacking a family car to borrow. I would wash it, wax it, and fill it full of gas. Then when I was finished with it, I would leave it as close as possible to where I stole it. I did this so often that one of the columnists at the local newspaper put a paragraph in his column titled "Steal My Car Please" because so many people got their cars back clean and full of gas. Then one night, I got a good lesson in planning by stealing a car on the wrong street. I rolled it away from the house, jumped the coil to hot, then proceeded to try to bump start it on a street that had too little slope. I would push it as fast as I could, run up, jump in, and kick it into gear but just didn't have the speed to start the engine. After yet another failed attempt while I was sitting in the car, a police cruiser pulled up behind me. Because of my years of observing others, I understood that people will believe any front fostered so long as the person doing so exuded a calm confidence, whether that person was calm inside or not. I put on my calmest front then jumped out of the car. I approached the officer with a big smile on my face. I made a joke about English cars being wired by "Lucas the Prince of Darkness" (Lucas made English electrical components, the joke was "why do the English drink warm beer... Lucas refrigerators"). He believed all was as it appeared so offered to push me to get it started. I am pretty sure he didn't tell anyone once the car came up stolen the next day.

That was, by comparison, at worst a minor joyriding charge, and I was a juvenile. Now, however, I was an adult committing felonies every day. This is not to say I didn't take pains to limit my exposures, quite the contrary. I covered my bases by continuing to run possible scenarios in my head to identify potential problems. Once identified, I would try to mitigate or avoid them entirely. In fact, as you will learn, I went to great lengths to avoid pitfalls that I had identified through this process.

In my earlier years, I learned that if you believe, others will believe. A confident demeanor makes it less likely they will suspect you are not what you are trying to appear to be. I also learned that there are times when one has no choice but to kill.

Around that time, I began sourcing fake IDs. In the beginning, I paid a friend proficient with the equipment of the day to produce birth certificates with made-up names and the required raised stamps.

These worked for a time to get state driver's licenses, which I received from a few different states. Mostly the ones that would give you the license that day rather than mailing it. This to avoid having to get a local address, which came with the danger of a stakeout should one be discovered. For the most part, I found that few states would check the records to see if these births were actually recorded in those states. This would change.

I began to realize that if I was ever going to get out of this business before being put in jail, I would need to make more. The best way to do this was for me to find a connection who was closer to the source or import directly from a source country. I asked the guys who I had helped with the Thai Stick. They turned me on to a guy in Florida who was well connected. At that time, Florida was ground zero for smuggling everything. I got Sam, a friend who had sailed some boats in, and we flew down to Florida. Once there, I connected with Donald, the new supplier. He did have good Colombian weed at a good price; however, my read on him was that he was way over his head despite his attempts to convince me otherwise. I found out later that he was supposedly Meyer Lansky's accountant's son, grew up wealthy so had never been through trial by fire. I did my best to advise Donald of the things he was doing that could get us busted, in the most non-threatening way I could. Unfortunately, as I have found over and over, people who reach adulthood sheltered from the street never have or can acquire any street sense. A few years later, Donald would travel to San Francisco with a quantity of coke. While staying at a nice hotel on the Embarcadero, he proceeded to sell out of his room. Without warning, a couple guys forced their way into the room and relieved him of $750,000. He then traveled up to Tahoe, where I was, saying that I was one of the only people who knew he was there. He wanted me to take a lie detector test. I told him to stop watching so much TV, refused, then reminded him that he was hanging out in a hotel room with people coming and going all day. He was likely robbed by the housekeeper's boyfriend or brother. I had warned him about this before.

I was acutely aware that in this business you had to take calculated risks all the time, so must anticipate the potential for unexpected results when doing anything or suffer the consequences. I decided to proceed despite my misgivings about Donald's lack of experience, thinking the risk to be low. This was a mistake that would cost me later.

Sam and I went out to used car lots to purchase a used car. This was so we would not be driving out of Florida with out-of-state plates or in a rental (both red flags). The interstates in those days, as they are today, were crawling with police looking for anything unusual. We also picked up a toolbox, some spare parts like a fuel pump, starter, belts, hoses, a tire plug kit, and jumper cables. I had come to understand that you can never prepare for every eventuality, so your best insurance was your own ingenuity and ability to think under pressure. It did, however, help if you had spares. Next, we bought a Pop-Up camping trailer. Light so it could be towed by the car we bought. Also, because it had a toilet and a kitchen, it was considered a residence. A residence, unlike a motor vehicle, required a search warrant before law enforcement could legally search it. A tidy bit of information that would save my older brother from jail on a later trip.

We loaded up and left for California, never speeding, never stopping by having one sleep while the other drove. Pausing only occasionally for food and fuel until a couple of the little tires on the trailer blew. We were able to replace them en route without incident. Continuing through Colorado, we pulled into a gas station at night while going through the Cheyenne pass. It was reportedly 18 degrees below zero with the wind chill so when our tires cooled from traveling they froze to the pavement. Not wishing to risk tearing the tread off, I approached some other cars that were there only to find they too were stuck. I asked if the station jockey had any salt or antifreeze only to be told he didn't. You would think in a place where it was this cold often that a gas station near the freeway would? I approached him to ask for myself. I was told the same so I asked if there was a liquor store nearby. He directed me to one within walking distance. I fetched a gallon of cheap Vodka then freed everyone so we all were on our way. Don't know why no one else thought of this or that gasoline would have worked too if Jockey boy had not refused to allow it (risk of fire or some such silliness). Unexpectedly, there was a silver lining because all of these cars stayed close to us for quite a distance creating a kind of buffer shield from law enforcement. I guess they felt safer continuing near us as the conditions got worse with the increasing altitude approaching the summit.

The rest of the trip went off without incident. Sam and I rolled into Tahoe City after 2 days & 16 hours. Tahoe was increasingly becoming a haven for smugglers and drug dealers so we, as you might imagine, had friends there. The next day we skirted around the agricultural stop after Truckee on I-80 then headed to the Bay Area.

I would continue with this proven method for a time even enlisting my older Brother (who I did not grow up with) to drive. I put him in a pickup truck that had been modified to have a bed, toilet, and hot plate over a space that could be filled with weed. The work and research were done by my little brother (again who I did not grow up with) who also registered it in Colorado. This because we felt that it being between Florida and California the plates would garner less scrutiny. Unfortunately, if the driver did not obey the law, no amount of planning would protect him. My older brother was pulled over for speeding with a load of weed. He then, against my explicit instructions, gave them permission to search. It doesn't matter how good you set it up if your people don't stick to the plan.

Fortunately, because of the steps taken by my little brother, my lawyers were able to not only spring my older brother but get the truck back. I was told that it was just a matter of time before he would be re-arrested, so I arranged to fly him out of state to the Pacific Northwest where he hid, working as a logger for some time.

This unfortunate event not only cost me cash but also burned my program. I began casting about for my next plan.

Finally, I once again contacted George from the jewelry business who had helped me before. I had been voluntarily paying him a small percentage of every deal I did with Al, so he was more than willing to help. George introduced me to a guy who was going under the name Leo Sunshine. I have no idea what his real name was since he was already wanted and on the run from previous activities. He had a contact for Hashish in India with a plan to get it to Mexico. He needed me to take it home into the US.

His plan was to go to New Delhi, India, load up, then travel by air from New Delhi to Frankfurt, Germany. Instead of entering Germany, we would stay in the "Transit Lounge" to board another flight to Montreal, Canada. Once there, we would again transit through the lounge to board a flight dubbed the farmworker special. This flight departed from Montreal to Acapulco, Mexico every Friday night. It was full of Mexican workers traveling home for the weekend to return Monday morning. As such, customs, when arriving in Mexico, consisted of one sleepy guard who would not search anyone since the flight was coming from Canada (not a source country) and was full of nationals.

Leo's plan had a number of flaws I will mention later.

Once in Mexico, we would travel to Tijuana to meet up with my crew. My guys would come in 1965 ex-PG&E Chevy trucks with wetsuits and surfboards. The beaches south of Tijuana are to this day a popular surfing destination. The pickups had what are called "split rim" spares. These are spare tires hung under the rear bed, mounted on rims that could be disassembled in the field to change tires without special equipment. We would fill the spare tires with hash, remount the tires, inflate them, wash them (for dogs), then replace them under the bed. The guys would get into the water to cover their wetsuits and boards with sand then head for the border. The idea being that if the contraband was discovered, their defense would be "anyone could have put it there intending to follow them home and steal it back later." Not sure if this defense strategy would have worked because we never got caught. Two of these guys, Jono and Jimmy, would later become important members of my crew.

Leo and I flew to New Delhi multiple times over the next year, buying hash and bringing it back in this way. We would stick the product to the mirror in our hotel room. If it stayed for an hour, we accepted its quality, so purchased more. Despite running successfully, I was increasingly concerned by our having to have everything go perfectly every time with all the various stages of the trip. On one occasion, for example, I was sitting in the transit lounge in Montreal when I saw, through the glass doors to enter the country, my bags come up on the luggage roundabout. The handlers had screwed up, failing to place them on our departing flight as the tags directed. I got up, walked over, grabbed my bags, then walked towards the inspection area. After showing my passport, the inspector just waived me through. I walked to the airline counter to check them in again. I had the pleasure of smuggling an extra time that trip, but it could have gone much differently. I wanted some fallback tools for unexpected things like this. The most troubling flaws were in areas where our program could be spotted by an alert travel agent or customs officer. The two biggest were:

1. At that time, travelers booked their flights through travel agents or directly with the airline. It was very suspicious for an American to book such a circuitous route home. Even if you booked each leg with a different agent, you must use the same name for the checked luggage. I was concerned we might be flagged for scrutiny at some point. The various Customs Agencies did get passenger lists with final destinations on each. Next;

2. India, at that time, had a "Closed Currency" to keep its wealthy citizens from taking their assets out of the country. Consequently, there was customs leaving India as well as arriving. A "Closed Currency" is one that is not traded on exchanges outside the country, so the Rupee effectively had no value outside of India.

The closed currency policy did have a silver lining in that any negotiable form of foreign currency in large denomination could be sold on the black market in India for as much as a 10% premium over face value. This was because significant assets could be hidden, so carried out by those wishing to. Remember we were carrying in hundreds of thousands of dollars to buy hash each trip.

I ran scenario after scenario through my head until I finally devised a plan that I felt solved all the problems of entering, exiting, and travel. I decided that instead of trying to not be noticed, we would "Hide in plain sight." In order to pull this off, I would need to create a plausible but fictional branch of Government. At the time, I was hearing our Government workers abroad being labeled as the "Diplomatic Corps" in news broadcasts. This was simply a descriptive term, not a branch of the government. It fit the bill mainly because State Department representatives traveled between varied destinations that were not necessarily related all the time.

CHAPTER 5

THE UNITED STATES DIPLOMATIC CORPS. OR "THEY HAVE CATTLE PRODS IN MEXICO TOO"

I had in my possession my father's old briefcase, which had in it his State Department Top Secret Clearance card. I brought this to my fake ID guy, provided him with my picture and that of my partner, Leo. He then produced cards for each of us. I found passport covers that had embossed in gold the American eagle with the words "United States of America" above. Next, I found a printer specializing in leather. He matched the font to add "Diplomatic Corp" below. These passport covers were bright red. I was aware that real diplomatic passports were black; however, I calculated that the agents I was likely to show these to would not know the truth and would be impressed by the red. I attached the State

Department cards inside so they would be the first thing seen. Next, I found very stout dark brown leather luggage that looked like something the government would provide, bought a number of pieces, then had them also printed on the side with "United States of America Diplomatic Corp." in gold. For the cherry on top, I attached some large (3.5 inches) circular enamel seals I had found, showing the American Eagle above the lettering. The seals being dished out delivered a look of substance with quality worthy of such an important agency representing such a powerful country. I then picked up red, white, and blue luggage straps to ensure the bags didn't pop open when being handled. This would also make it difficult for handlers to easily open them to steal.

In order to complete the picture, I decided some kind of standardized outfit was required. I found dark blue blazers with gold-colored American Eagle buttons and built around them white dress shirts, gray slacks, black dress shoes, black leather belts with red, white, and blue striped ties for us both. Finally, I had brass name tags engraved with our names and USDC to be worn on the left chest.

To deal with the difficulty of obtaining tickets, I bought a subscription to the Official Airline Guide (OAG), which was like an old phone book but included all flights for all airlines with schedules, destinations, etc. I borrowed a travel agent's IATA number (a girl I had met and started dating during my research) so I could book flights directly myself.

This worked like a charm both coming and going for quite a number of trips. Eventually, we began to wish we had more capacity, so I enlisted Jono who was by then also selling for me. Leo, my partner, found a couple of civilians who fit the bill and wanted to make extra money. I outfitted each of them. I even bought a Ben Hogan red, white, and blue golf bag to stuff full. Everything went smoothly. We were in New Delhi, loaded, waiting for our departure flight, when in the morning I picked up the English version of the New Delhi Times. On the front page was a picture of the Nepalese Temple Balls we had been buying along with the caption "largest drug bust in New Delhi history." It continued to read "believed to be selling to foreigners staying at one of the InterContinental hotels." This development was of major concern because in India at that time when you checked into a hotel they kept your passport until you checked out. Their way of ensuring payment I suppose. This meant that the authorities need only collect all passports of foreigners then show them to the dealers. The dealers were sure to pick us out since torture was a common practice at that time in India.

I figured we had at most twelve hours to get out of India, so I pulled out my OAG looking for flights that would at least get us to Mexico, from where I knew I could get us home. I was able to find and book tickets for us all, leaving for Madrid, Spain, that afternoon. We would transit lounge in Madrid, Spain, then continue on to Cancun, Mexico, finally landing in the early morning. I checked, and there was a US consulate in Cancun which supported our cover, but there was a problem. Spain was, at that time, a source country for heroin. Cancun, Mexico, was a duty-free port, so this was going to be rough, still, not as rough as a cattle prod up the rectum.

I called the airline in New Delhi, told them I was from the embassy, and I wanted to alert them that we had a group of our people leaving for Spain that afternoon. I then asked that the airline please do everything possible to facilitate their departure. We checked out of the hotel, went to the airport, checked our bags, went through immigration to leave. We proceeded to the luggage area where our bags were to be searched for wealth being smuggled out. Normally they did not search a group of official foreigners, but I was concerned they might be looking for drugs leaving given the bust. Fortunately, when we reached the customs area, our bags had already been placed on the plane. We took off for Spain.

Jono, Leo, and I were aware that this was only one hurdle. Mexico could be a shit show. Leo's couriers, I found out, were in the dark having been told we had some customs agent named Juan on the payroll. Just what I needed: amateurs who would likely panic in a pinch.

Our flight landed in Cancun, Mexico, on time at 4:30 AM local time. I had instructed all members of our group to go to the bathroom, freshen up, and change to a fresh shirt before landing. I wanted to present a serious, professional, no-nonsense group of US State Department diplomats from the moment we entered the airport, knowing as I did that most countries had cameras surveilling arriving passengers. This is so customs agents can spot any who seem uncomfortable or out of place.

When we finally entered the luggage claim and inspection area, it was pandemonium. There were women crying, children screaming, with custom agents literally slicing open bags. Leo's civilians kept asking "which one is Juan." As I positioned myself to collect our bags when they came up on the belt, Jono leaned over to me and quietly asked "what we were going to do." I calmly told him "we are going to walk out of here." I had already concluded that our best chance was to play it to the hilt. I had Jono go around to collect everyone's passport and tell them that when I started walking, they should line up behind me and follow, eyes forward, stopping for no one. While he did this, I piled all of our bags on a cart, then paid one of the luggage help kids $20 instructing him to push the cart to the doors outside without stopping.

I set off at a relaxed pace towards the exit doors with the cart piled high being pushed to my left. To the right at the luggage inspection stations, various agents called us over, saying they could take us there. This I ignored, continuing forward. Before we reached the doors, a big guy I took to be the Chief, who had been watching this unfold from behind a podium, stepped out in front of me and demanded our passports. I gave him the red leather stack. When he opened the one on top, mine, he read the Top Secret clearance card. He then opened the second. After a moment, he looked up at me and said, "are you all State Department?" I answered yes, he thought for a second more, then waved us through.

I loaded us into a van and directed the driver to a hotel I knew from having vacationed there some time earlier. It was not until we were in the room that anyone but me spoke.

I immediately arranged flights for our 3 couriers back to the US direct that afternoon. My concern was that Cancun, being a small place, someone might mention to the US consular staff that we had arrived. Of course, this could ring bells, causing the police to come looking. Splitting us up eliminated one description to search for, that being a group of 5 Americans. It also got Leo's civilians and Jono away from us and the drugs. I then booked Leo and me a flight up to the US border the following evening. I contacted Jimmy, who was also by this time selling for me in California. I asked him to pick up the truck that had been returned earlier from my brother's arrest, then drive down to pick us up at the Mexican airport. I promised him a good cash payment with the truck for running a few errands for me before picking us up. He was to pick up two-wheeled carts of the type towed behind motorcycles, then scout the US side of the border for a spot where we could be picked up after crossing. I also required he bring me a compass and heading to the pick-up spot. Finally, he was to find a place at the border fence on the Mexico side where we could cross unnoticed.

I have to give Jimmy credit for a job well done on such short notice. When we arrived at the airport with our bags stuffed with hash, he was there waiting. He had everything requested. He drove us to a dark area at the border fence where we threw a blanket (also provided by him) over the razor wire 10 feet above, tossed our bags and the carts over, then followed ourselves.

We set off walking while dragging 800 lbs of luggage and Hashish through the high desert. The one thing I forgot to request was warm clothing. The high desert routinely drops below freezing at night even in summer. We were dressed in business attire ill-suited for such a trip. I navigated as we continued but was becoming increasingly concerned by our slow progress pulling the carts through the sand. We needed to meet Jimmy early in the morning at the rendezvous spot which was twelve miles inland. He would not wait long, fearing the border patrol might get suspicious.

Finally, as the sky was beginning to get lighter with the sunrise, directly in front of us was the campground. I had hit it dead on. We went to the highest camping area which allowed a view of any incoming traffic. I instructed Leo to change into a clean shirt. We didn't want to look as though we spent all night crossing the border. No sooner had we cleaned up when here comes Jimmy right on time. We put the luggage under the bed then headed for the airport to catch our flight to the Bay Area. As we left the campground on a two-lane dirt road coming in the opposite direction, we see a US Border Patrol Ram Charger. I put on my best relaxed happy face, joking with my fellow passengers. When we passed, the agent looked us over but didn't stop us. We checked the bags at the airline and boarded without further incident.

CHAPTER 6

I NEED A VACATION, I THINK!

Over the years, I would go on adventures periodically, such as flying down to the Yucatan when I heard that a fisherman had discovered sharks sleeping in caves. I knew from my Marine Biology studies that lacking bony gill covers to pump water for their gills, sharks could never stop swimming or they would drown. I beat Jacques Cousteau by two weeks.

Now, home, I decided I needed a vacation, so I booked a flight to Maui, Hawaii. I had read about a sunken submarine sitting intact on the sandy bottom in 140 feet of water. The US Navy had scuttled it years earlier to use for training. It had become an artificial reef of sorts. Once there, I booked passage on a dive boat going to the wreck. In due course, we arrived. Being the organized type, who was always ready first, I jumped in and swam to the marker buoy. Once I reached the buoy, I looked down to see if the wreck was visible from the surface (unlikely). I could not see the wreck but did see one Pacific Whitetip Shark of about 6 feet in length.

I had a custom camera rig I had fabricated which carried a Nikonos 3 underwater camera over a Nikonos 5, one with a macro lens, the other with a micro lens, each with its own strobe light. I lifted this rig out of the water to set the F-stop to take a picture of the shark. By the time I put the camera back in the water, there were more than 50 similar sharks circling me. I know the number from one of the pictures I took. It showed 15 sharks, and when I multiplied its lens range to 360 degrees, it came out to 50. I found out later that the Navy had been training on the wreck the day before. When they left, they tossed their garbage. The sharks heard my splash and reacted like it was the dinner bell. The dive boat operators busily got everyone else out of the water, telling me after that all they could see of me was dozens of fins.

I have never been one to panic, preferring instead to try to figure a solution. I decided if I was going to be eaten, I was going to get pictures, so I focused and pressed the shutter. Instantly, as the strobe light flashed, the sharks backed off a little. I had a knife, but here was a tool I could exploit. I began slowly swimming towards the boat, clicking pictures, setting off the strobes. As I went, the sharks became increasingly accustomed to the flash, plus the strobes were taking longer and longer to charge up because the batteries were being drained. As I got nearer to the boat, the boldest of the pack began making test runs at me. They would swim very fast towards me to veer off at the last minute. I believe they were testing to see if I posed a danger to them before attacking. In one of only three pictures that came out, you can see one going away who had just passed with one heading directly in to make his run along with many others swimming in the circle. The last picture I took was of my flipper pushing one away as I climbed up the boat ladder.

So much for a relaxing vacation! I was ready to go back to work.

When Leo contacted me to make another trip to India, I told him we had run that smuggle long enough. It was time to retire it before someone got wise (if they hadn't already). He disagreed and was successful one more time. After that, I refused to risk my people again to get it over the Mexican border. He then paid me to set up a Dodge Ram Charger to look like a border patrol vehicle, which he wanted bulletproofed. I suppose he was going to drive across, so I outfitted the Ram Charger then waited for him to instruct where I should deliver it. I never got that call. When he tried the smuggle again, they were waiting for him in Canada. He was arrested. He would later ask me through his attorney to break him out, which I did not feel I owed him. I would find out a couple of years later that he had escaped only to be caught doing something else in Costa Rica. When attempting yet another escape, Leo took a hostage. The police shot both of them dead.

Back in California and without an ongoing program, I busied myself middling some product. I had earlier helped my then-girlfriend and her gay partner, Brad, who was the mutual friend who introduced she and I, set up a vintage clothing store. They specialized in everything from original "silky" Hawaiian shirts & Japanese silk Kimonos to cowboy shirts from the 30's and 40's. At one time, I think I had the best collection of vintage Hawaiian shirts on the planet. Having grown up in San Francisco, I was comfortable with the gay community. In fact, my first girlfriend in high school was gay. In those days, it was sometimes easier for her to have a stand-in "boyfriend" to fend off potential suitors and those that hate. Later I was a major supplier to the gay community through a well-connected guy I had met through Brad. Because of this, I learned that the gay clubs were fun. First of all, those guys know how to party. Also, there are a lot of women in those clubs and not all are gay. When I told my friends about this, they would ask what I would do if a man bought me a drink. I would answer that I would thank him, drink the drink, and not fuck him. Women have been doing this forever.

Another friend, Jeff, who backed the vintage clothing store venture with me, who I also met through Brad, would later become one of my oldest friends. He was in the same business as I was but specialized in Acid and made very good money. He introduced me to (or maybe it was my girlfriend) another guy who supplied the movie industry. This guy became a regular customer of mine as well. These are examples of market expansion in that business.

All fine, but now I needed to identify and set up my next enterprise. I got in touch with Donald in Florida. I had previously bought weed from him so wanted to see if he could get me coke as well. He said he could, so I was off to Florida. I carried with me a Samsonite briefcase that I had modified to have a hidden compartment. I did this by taking two cases apart, shaving the plastic top half to fit into the other unshaved top half, leaving enough room for a quantity of coke. This was needed because a few years earlier the FAA started requiring bags be searched when going to the departure gates because of a rash of hijackings.

Travel to and from Florida carried with it extra risk due to the increasingly violent cocaine market and the government's war on drugs. I had to be careful to avoid fitting the profile of a person transporting drugs in order to get past the security check. To do this, I flew from a small airport North of Miami (where I had observed relaxed screening for drugs, money & weapons) to Atlanta, Georgia. This allowed me to arrive in Atlanta already in the secure area of the airport so I could simply walk to my California departure gate. The first leg went as planned. I was sitting at the gate for my flight to California when suddenly two undercover police officers came running around the corner obviously looking for someone or something. They immediately locked on me, approached, sat down on either side of me, then showed me their DEA badges. They physically lifted me to my feet, saying I had to come with them. We walked across the center aisle to the opposite empty gate. We went around a corner to a door which they opened to reveal a small office with a desk and a chair.

One agent sat behind the desk, with the other standing slightly behind to my left. The door was on my right. The one behind the desk demanded my ID. He asked if he could search my briefcase. I said no. He then asked what the purpose of my trip was. Next, he asked, "Was I carrying any drugs or large amounts of cash?" I told him I was a jewelry courier, which was why I did not have a key for the briefcase. The ID I gave him matched the name on my ticket. It was a genuine driver's license; it just wasn't my name. I also had in my wallet various items to make it appear that this was a real person. These included a pilot's license, hunting license, gym membership card, etc., most printed by my forger friend. They asked me if they could pat me down, which I allowed, all while I was trying to figure out how I was going to separate myself from the briefcase. I wanted to accomplish this before they brought a dog up to get probable cause for a search. I was looking for an opportunity. I knew if one presented itself, I would have to act fast.

I then heard the announcement calling for the boarding of my flight. I asked if I was under arrest, to which the agent behind the desk answered, "Not yet." I responded, saying, "Then I am going to board my flight," and reached for the briefcase. The agent standing put his hand on the case, saying they were not going to let me take the case unless I let them search it.

Before they could react, I said, "Keep it," and walked out the door. I went across the aisle to board my flight. I think I was so quick that they were taken by surprise. This is important because once I was out in the public area, they could not lie and say I had given permission to search. If I had, they would have found the coke and would not have allowed me to leave that little office. This then constitutes illegal search & seizure since they are not allowed to take or search your property without permission from you or probable cause that a crime was committed. Any evidence found would, therefore, be illegally obtained, so excluded from use in any trial. My checking onto the flight would be irrefutable evidence of this.

The steward closed the aircraft door, and the plane began to back out of the gate when the Captain came on to say we had a small maintenance issue so would have to return to the gate but would be on our way once again shortly. Once docked, the very gay steward came up to me, obviously excited. He told me there was someone who wanted to talk to me at the doorway. When I walked there, one of the DEA agents was standing at the threshold, very agitated. He ordered me to get off the plane. I said no! He then ordered me to produce my ID. They had obviously forced the briefcase, found the coke, then checked on my ID. When they found it to have been obtained a month earlier with no history, they must have realized they not only could not arrest me but now did not even know who I was. Anxious to get in the air, I needled him a bit. He threw my ID in my face and said, "We will see you in San Francisco." This was a nonstop flight. He stood there in the window watching us taxi out.

I had around 6 hours to figure out a way to get by them. If they were able to arrest me, I would be found not guilty for the reasons mentioned above, but I would do so from the inside of an Atlanta Jail. I would be considered a flight risk. No southern judge would grant bail for a suspect who had access to fake IDs.In trying to understand where I had picked up the heat that focused their attention on me, I kept coming back to Donald, who had supplied the product. I had had misgivings about his experience and street sense before but had decided the risk was low. Now I was racking my brain trying to figure out why I had not seen this possibility when running scenarios in my head. I decided that he must have been under some kind of surveillance that allowed me to be flagged so that when I checked in for the flight to Atlanta, they were alerted.

Years later, in a court filing where the DEA was trying to keep some cash they had taken from my home, they used this incident to try to convince the court the cash was ill-gotten. Surprisingly, they recounted the incident accurately, saying only that when they met the plane in San Francisco, they were unable to contact me. No mention of how I was picked out for scrutiny. They also did not explain why they could not "contact" me. The following is the first time I have shared how I was able to avoid them.

At that time, when incoming commercial flights docked at the gate, the flight crew would exit first. The ground crew would then get the passengers off. This is unlike today where the flight crew also helps passengers to de-plane. Also common then as now, all members of the flight crew wore a uniform. In those days, this usually included a jacket or blazer. During the flight, I befriended the Stewart, eventually convincing him to sell me his uniform jacket in exchange for cash. When the plane docked, the flight crew lined up at the door to exit. When the door was opened, they filed out. I simply slipped in behind them with my uniform jacket, then walked past the agents waiting at the end of the hallway. Once around the corner, I threw the jacket in a trash can and I was in the wind.

A couple of days later, I went to the mail drop I used for mail and phone messages. They had two rows of cubbyholes marked for each person with the top row marked "in" and the second marked "delivered." The girl behind the desk was unusually excited. She told me that a detective had called leaving a message for me to have my attorney call him. I asked her to please leave that message in the "in" box. This was because I did not want them to be able to say I was notified which could possibly be used to toll the Statute of Limitations if a warrant had been issued. Statutes of Limitations are usually either 5 or 7 years depending upon the offense. Once that time has passed, the offender can no longer be prosecuted unless it can be shown he or she was out of the country or was aware there was a warrant but chose not to come in.

By this time, I was already taking steps to be under the radar while engaging in illegal activities, hence the fake ID. I surmised the only way they could have figured out who I was would have been fingerprints. I knew that inside the briefcase there were none because I always wore gloves when handling drugs, but it would look suspicious to check in at the airport wearing gloves carrying a briefcase. The mail drop was the address on my driver's license. Plus, the DMV required fingerprints when applying for a driver's license.

I did have a good explanation of how my fingerprints could have been on the briefcase without my being there. At the time, I had a side business manufacturing these briefcases for jewelry dealers or those who carried cash and drugs. I could have used this as part of a defense to create reasonable doubt.

I made an appointment with a good attorney familiar with Federal drug cases. He advised that I had a good chance of being found innocent without admissible evidence so should contact them to see if there was a warrant out. I considered this for a moment then came to the conclusion that, having just lost a sizable amount of cash, if I went in I would likely be fighting from within jail. This meant I could not earn to pay bills. I would have to be represented by a Public Defender. I had seen many cases handled by Public Defenders turn out poorly for those being defended. I had no confidence in their abilities so informed my attorney I was not going in. He said he had never seen anyone decide to go this route so calmly. I did run into him again many years later. He told me that in his career I was the only one he knew of to successfully take this route.

CHAPTER 7

UNDER THE RADAR

The first order of business was to somehow get actual ID, preferably a US passport, in other than my name. At the time, you needed a Social Security Card, a birth certificate, and a picture ID to apply for a passport. This was problematic because for passports, the birth certificates were checked for authenticity. I found this out by applying for one with a forged birth certificate. They did send me an SS card on my real driver's license from a fake birth certificate. I took these to the Passport office in the Federal building in San Francisco knowing that if you showed them an airline ticket for very soon, they would issue overnight. When I returned to collect my passport, the agent at the desk very casually told me it would be a few minutes, not long. Suspicious, I told him I would just go call my employer to tell him I would be late. I left immediately. I needed the passport, and the agent was so smooth that I was not entirely sure it was a trap, so I enlisted Brad, the same gay friend who had introduced me to my current girlfriend friend, to pick it up. Brad was very gay with dyed red hair. He was also someone I knew to be trustworthy. I correctly surmised that given the trials that gay people of the time had to endure, he would likely be able to hold up if things went south. When he went to pick up the passport, he was immediately detained, then put into an interrogation room. As we had rehearsed, he told them that some "cute boy" he had met in a bar asked him to do this favor. He then ad-libbed, telling one of the agents he was cute, asking when he got off work. As you might expect, the agents couldn't get him out of there fast enough.

Treasury agents then got the license plate number of the car that I had taken the driving test in, in New Mexico. They visited the owner who was my older sister. The Agents had no idea who I was but showed her a picture which she immediately identified as me. She was 12 years older than I and again I had not grown up with her. Now I had the DEA and Treasury looking for me.

I still needed to earn, so it became paramount that I solve the ID problem. It was fairly common knowledge in my circles that in past years people would find a baby born in the correct year range that had died so they could take that identity. Unfortunately, by this time, the government was taking steps to eliminate this avenue. To begin with, when a baby died even if from another state, its birth certificate would be stamped deceased. I discovered that this system was imperfect in that only those born in states close to the state in which they died would be routinely notified so if born in a state across the country there was a good chance the Birth Certificate was clean. Then was the problem of obtaining the needed information to allow one to mail in for a copy. Most states required the date of birth, mother's maiden name, county of the birth, and a small fee. I found that in California almost no recorders maintained the old birth/death record books, having converted to microfiche or film. In addition, none of them would allow someone to come in to leaf through the records. A person had to present at the counter, tell them the Birth Date, name, mother's maiden name etc. and the requesting person's relationship to the individual whose birth certificate was being requested.

After some research, I found that San Jose still had the old books. I then spent time in the recorder's office, ostensibly researching chain of title for property, so I could observe the way they conducted the counter. I found that they usually had young interns who would be left to man the counter every day while the officers went to lunch. I just needed a convincing story to get by these interns. At the time, one of the front-page news stories was the revelation that in the 1950s, our government had released germs offshore to be blown inland in a clandestine effort to quantify the effects of a potential germ warfare attack. In the 1950s, of course, we were in the depths of the Cold War, with nuclear bomb drills in the schools and paranoia rampant. I made up a convincing law firm name, then had cards printed with my phony name as an attorney. I put on an appropriate suit, then as soon as the regular staff left for lunch, I presented my ID and card to the interns. I told them my firm was preparing a suit for a number of families who lost babies in the 1950s. To do this, I needed to go over the records to see how many might have been affected. They put me at a desk behind the counter with the books, and for almost an hour, I went over death records year by year, looking for young babies who died in California but were not residents of California. Surprisingly, there were a few each year. By the time the regular staff returned and threw me out, I had a dozen candidates. All info needed was included on the death certificates.

After setting up remote mail drops at various locations, I began ordering Birth Certificates. It was always tense when checking the boxes because it was possible one of these was stamped deceased and the law was waiting to nab me. I would watch from a distance looking for stakeouts, but every one came in without a hitch.

I now had the means to obtain all the supporting documents and ultimately passports. Once acquired, I put each identity in a different safe deposit box with some amount of cash in case of emergency. When I was going on a smuggle, I would visit one of the boxes, deposit the ID I was living under, then leave with the new ID. This system kept me safe for the rest of my career until I again surfaced as myself, the statute of limitations having run out. This system also would allow me to live a parallel legal life working as a carpenter, then eventually buying and selling properties all under assumed identities.

Next, I asked around my circle for anyone who had a connection for Cocaine in South America. One friend came through. He was Jimmy, the very same guy who had earlier dropped me off at the Mexican Border with bags of Hashish. He had been to Lima, Peru, so had friends there who could supply what we needed. In figuring out how to get the product from Lima, Peru, to the United States, it is important to understand the normal commerce or travel between countries being considered. If you try to travel or import in a way that is unusual, you will likely garner unwanted attention. I found that Lima, Peru, had a large Japanese population. Coincidentally, so did Mexico City. An American flying from Lima to Mexico City would be suspicious, especially as Peru is a source country; a person carrying a Japanese passport would not. As it happened, when home, I liked to go to the Japanese baths in Japan Town San Francisco. There was also a Japanese hotel there that I had used often enough that the woman who managed the desk and I had become friendly. She was Korean, named Eiko, was much older and had complained that she saw no way she could ever retire on the pay she received. Her Japanese husband had died suddenly, leaving little savings, but because of him, she carried a Japanese passport. I suggested I knew a way she could retire comfortably within a year. After I described my plan, she agreed. I would create Samsonite suitcases much like my briefcases with a hidden compartment and load them up so she could carry them from Lima to Mexico City. Before her arrival, I flew to Lima with Jimmy to meet his contact. This turned out to be a wild ride through the city at night as we followed his contact's directions. He was apparently very paranoid about meeting new people, plus the police were cracking down at that time. We finally connected, throwing money and product through car windows, then leaving quickly. Not ideal, but the product was good. Also after this first sale, he became more comfortable.

Eiko arrived in Lima and checked in to the hotel on time. We quickly set to packaging the product, vacuum sealing it in plastic in one room. We would then carry it to a different room where the bags were washed to minimize contamination of the luggage for dogs. The coke was then sealed in the luggage compartments with special screws I had manufactured to look like the original rivets that held the bags together. The compartments tapered from the back to front so if a suspicious agent squeezed the front where he could with his thumb and forefinger, there was no space. In the back where the hinges are, it was impossible to do this. I gave Eiko back the bags, and we went to the airport. Eiko was a rather rotund woman, so I instructed her to wear a loose flowing dress with a money belt beneath. The money belt containing little but a small amount of cash would cause a visible bulge in her outer garment.

Jimmy flew home, leaving Eiko and me to continue to Mexico City. When we arrived in Mexico City, she lined up with her bags for inspection. I lined up a couple of people back to run interference should it be needed. When she was up, the customs agent immediately had a female agent escort her to a room for search. She was led away screaming insults in Korean the whole way, and when she returned, they passed her with little further inspection.

This program would continue for almost a year with many profitable trips. It ended when Jimmy, after purchasing, dove into one of the bags. He got so high he became difficult to handle. After I took it away, Jimmy started screaming in our hotel. Fearing he would bring the authorities down on us, Jono, who I had brought down with me to help, stuck his hand in Jimmy's mouth. Jimmy promptly bit down so hard that blood was pouring down Jono's arm. Despite this, Jono did not cry out. I stepped in and knocked Jimmy out. Now we had to keep Jimmy subdued until we were able to get safely out of the country with the product. Jono and I walked the groggy Jimmy through the lobby by putting our arms under his, so he seemed to be walking between us. We threw him into a cab, explaining he had had too much to drink. We then paid the driver $200 with instructions to take him as far away as possible and throw him out. We had relieved Jimmy of his passport, thinking it would take him a couple of days to get home. It took a week.

Turned out to be a good time to stop. I landed in Mexico City, then proceeded to customs to line up a few people behind Eiko, as usual. Not as usual, a curious agent started inspecting the suitcase while Eiko was off being searched. When I saw this, I played the rude American, complaining loudly that I had a plane to catch and "can't we hurry this up." The agent pushed her bags aside, waved the two people in front of me without search, and proceeded to thoroughly search me inside and out. I finally emerged to Eiko waiting for me at our hotel two and a half hours later, no worse for wear. I did think the agent who strip-searched me owed me a kiss before getting so intimate. Eiko, once home, retired comfortably.

CHAPTER 8

MARRIED

Now doing well, having made some money, I was looking to create new legal enterprises so I could get out of the business. I looked at buying an island in the Caribbean. I found they were not expensive. This, I found, was because they had no power or water on them. I put my mind to it and designed a Tidally Motivated electrical generation system. Typically, only wave-generated systems were being designed because although the tides created by the moon's gravity exert tremendous force pushing vast amounts of water, they only happen twice a day. Few islands in the Caribbean had significant wave action, so I looked for some way to store electrical energy created for use later. Unable to find a suitable system, I designed my own using off-the-shelf equipment. Once you have energy, you can get fresh water from the ocean through the process of reverse osmosis. This entails powering a high-pressure pump to force saltwater through a semi-permeable membrane which has holes large enough for H2O to pass but not large enough for the larger Sodium Chloride salt molecule. I have not yet had time or money to exploit these designs.

When I was between trips and not building or setting up my next program, I was out and about in a county which was becoming increasingly popular with Rock Stars and A-list celebrities. Marin County, just north of the Golden Gate Bridge, remains known for its beauty and laid-back atmosphere. In those days, it was known as a place where celebrities were treated as anyone else so had some anonymity when not on the road or making a movie. Because of this, I became friendly with more than a few, going to parties, even standing as best man for one lead guitar man's wedding. I would also sometimes fly band members to gigs. On these occasions, I needed to keep a low profile to avoid becoming affiliated with the band. It would not be good if my picture and/or name were published in the trades. The band members also practiced this using aliases like Seymore Butts and Imma

Hogge when checking into hotels to prevent fans or paparazzi from calling around to locate where they were staying. I also had to use an alias after some fans figured out I was a friend of the band then got my name. I would routinely check in as Dr. Richard Wahd (Dick to my friends).

At the same time, when I was home, I was buying houses to remodel and sell. I had broken up with my previous girlfriend, opting instead for a string of short-term relationships with girls far more beautiful than I deserved. One day I was driving down Second Street in San Rafael in a sweet 1970 Dino Ferrari that I had had for some time. I saw this beautiful girl riding a moped to the right side. I slowed to ask her to go out with me. She politely declined. Unconvinced, I swung my car over, blocking a number of lanes, and her, to say I was not going to move until she gave me her number. With cars backing up but curiously not honking, she gave in, reciting the number. This all while I was being actively searched for by law enforcement.

I was relieved to find that the number she gave me was real. We began to date. Shortly before this, I had been contacted by Theo, one of the old smugglers mentioned previously. He had a connection in Peru who owned a commercial foundry and wanted to do a smuggle. After traveling down and staying at Lalo, the connection's home with Theo, I returned to create a program. I made up a company name I believed sounded substantial, filed a fictitious name statement, opened a bank account, obtained an EIN (Employer Identification Number), then a business license. All based at a rented office in an industrial area across the bay in Emeryville using fake ID so it could not be traced to me. I then had Lalo in Peru begin sending container loads of big heavy cast iron "spider gears" used on trailers pulled behind Semi-trucks. When contract drivers haul trailers they don't own, they save their truck brakes by engaging the trailer brakes causing them to wear out quickly. This satisfied the first requirement of an import smuggle, i.e., the import had to make financial sense. Peru had large reserves of iron ore and few environmental restrictions so cast iron imported from there was profitable. I had Lalo, when filling out the customs declaration, say under payment type "Bank to Bank wire transfer." This satisfied the second requirement for an import smuggle, normal business banking was done through banks not in cash. The reason I knew the buttons we wanted to avoid was because another old smuggler, Thomas, had bribed a worker at the Oakland port to give him a copy of the pamphlet circulated annually by US customs outlining the things to look for. The next requirement was a bit harder. The importing company should have history; new importers from a source country were immediately suspect. To satisfy this, we imported a number of containers full of nothing but spider gears. I had to dispose of all of these so began selling just as the company represented it would and in fact was showing a nice profit.

At first, when my broker's agent picked up the containers, Customs would cut the seal placed in Peru and inspect the cargo. By the time we were ready to fill some of the Spider Gears with product, we were receiving the containers with the seal intact.

I booked a flight for Theo and me to Lima. I asked Jenna, my new girlfriend, to move into my house and take care of it with my dog for a couple of weeks. I gave her a wad of cash to cover any expenses and left. She did know my business by this time and, in fact, did know my real name.

When we arrived in Lima, we went directly to Lalo's house where he told us that the government was cracking down. This meant it was too dangerous to transport coke from Cuzco in the mountains to Lima. We rented a house outside Lima that coincidentally was owned by the chief of customs and settled in to wait. You didn't want to hang out in a hotel room because in these third world source countries, the housekeeping staff often reported to the police anything unusual that they saw. I went to great pains to look the part of a legitimate businessman. I would leave blueprints laying around, and I would leave early in the morning, not returning until late afternoon, all to give a particular impression. I did occasionally see some cowboy on the flight wearing a gold Rolex or something equally conspicuous. Not sure if it worked out for them. Theo and I picked up a couple of pellet guns to pass the time, seeing who could shoot the biggest cockroach. I couldn't call my Jenna for obvious reasons.

We worked at the foundry making spider gears that had a hollow hub with a spool that could be wrapped with product then slid down into the hollow. We would drill holes with special bits to slide pins to anchor the spools. Cast iron can be formulated so that it dulls normal drill bits. This prevents exploratory drilling by Customs. Once done, we would smear Devcon over the pins and seams. Devcon is an epoxy with as much as 90% metal powder mixed in so it can be sanded and painted. This allowed us to make the gears look like nothing had been done.

Finally, we are able to load the container for shipment. Theo, Lalo, and I placed the special spider gears to the rear with regular ones on substandard pallets in front. By the time it arrives, the front pallets will have collapsed, leaving thousands of pounds of jumbled spider gears in the way with no easy way to remove them.

When my taxi pulled up to my house, a month overdue, the lights were on. I went in to find Jenna playing with my dog. She was relaxed, not upset. Everything was as I left it. She even only spent a small amount of the cash for food and stuff. Not long after that, I asked Jenna to marry me.

We were married at the Corinthian Yacht Club

in Tiburon, California. There were over 300 guests. I couldn't help thinking that if the cops busted in (I was still living under cover), they would shut down the drug market in the United States for a while, there being so many major players there. I did have an airplane fueled and ready at the local airport in case I needed to leave quickly, but it wasn't needed.

I loved Jenna, but I am not sure I was "in love" with her. I just didn't know how to be in love. I had never witnessed it. I did what I thought one did when in love but always felt like I had missed. I made sure there was a fresh flower on her side of the bed every day for the 10+ years we were together. I even made her engagement ring with my own hands. To my friends, we presented as a devoted couple, but I sometimes felt I treated her like a cherished object rather than my friend or lover. I was aware of this lack of depth; I was just at a loss what to change or how. We never argued or even got angry at one another; it was just that all our interactions seemed as though we were both faking it. As the years flew by, rather than becoming more comfortable with her, I instead began to feel I didn't know her or how to relate to her on a personal level. On the surface, she was loving and supportive. I tried to be the same; it just seemed like we were both following a script. It may have been that my chosen profession at that time was so life and death it just didn't leave any common ground for she and I to grow. She couldn't relate to my world and I couldn't relate to anything else.

In the beginning, all this seemed like an exciting, even romantic, life. I felt like James Bond. I earned a professional racing license briefly driving for Mazda. Studied celestial navigation, built a 55-foot sailboat, and was going to sail around the world. I ended up sailing solo because no one wanted to go along. After I was knocked down running before a hurricane coming back from Cabo, I sold the boat. I then moved to offshore racing boats, which we used to offload from larger ships at high speeds with no lights, very dangerous. In time, with the romance of it fading, I began doing some contract flying bringing drugs or money across the border. This introduced a whole new set of problems. Out of necessity, I educated myself on the workings of turbine/jet engines as often I would find myself on some unimproved steaming jungle runway with 50-foot-high trees all around, getting into an airplane that showed high hours, had no maintenance logs, was overloaded with questionable fuel, plus too much cargo. Added to this was the crazy guy waving an automatic weapon telling me if I didn't take off soon, he would shoot me. I had to be a competent turbine mechanic, or I would be fertilizer. I had become, over the years, a good gas engine mechanic while building racing cars and restoring classic cars, a decent Diesel mechanic bringing in boats where if you had a problem the last people you wanted to call were the Coast Guard, and both when driving all manner of trucks or cars full of contraband across this country.

Now I needed to learn turbines. These are a totally different animal than what I was familiar with. To begin with, they are "Continuous Combustion Engines." This means that in the combustion chamber, the flame never goes out unlike piston engines whose cylinders each fire only one out of every four strokes. When turbines or jets shut down it is called a "flameout" because the flame literally has gone out. To run this way, these engines must be built to extremely tight clearances out of exotic materials that can handle extreme heat and continuous speeds from 45,000 to over 60,000 revolutions per minute. Add to this they must be built of differing alloys all of which expand and contract to differing degrees when exposed to heat. Finally, they must be balanced to very high RPM to prevent even the smallest vibrations. This is because any errant vibration under these extreme conditions has the potential to transform the engine into a Grenade spitting out metal bits at supersonic speeds. My life depended upon my ability to get the aircraft off the ground and running well enough to fly thousands of miles, overloaded, to land on a dirt, sand, or mud surface. Fortunately, I had been flying for years so had a good working knowledge of various aircraft along with their various systems. The main difference between jets and gas turbine engines is that the Jet motivates by thrust while the Turbine has a gearbox attached to drive propellers. The "Turbo Prop" can land or take off on shorter runways, is quieter and uses less fuel per mile. The Jet is faster, thirstier, and usually can carry more weight.

I would end up in turbo props most of the time. Once airborne, in one piece, I would be flying for hours with nav lights off, sometimes at low altitude, with limited fuel, and usually at night. Turbo props also usually have a less critical wing design, which allows them to fly slower without stalling. This was helpful because the

DEA had a fleet of Falcon Jets (fast but thirsty). If I suspected I was being tracked, I would slow down so they had to do circles to keep their speed up and still follow me. Eventually, they would get low on fuel so would break off the chase.

Upon arrival at the coordinates given, I then had to rely on the ground crew to have a runway cleared and leveled with generator-powered lights on either side.

The one time they were not there, I arrived low on fuel, finally having to ditch close to a road so I could hitch a ride away. For the next two weeks, the owners believed I had stolen the load, not believing my story over that of the ground crew. They were sending people after me until finally the story hit the papers. Not sure what happened to the ground crew and don't care any more than they did about my well-being.

There was a guy named Carlos Lederer who bought an island located on the way from South America to Florida so aircraft could be refueled. This allowed them to fly farther inland. It also made the use of smaller, less suspect aircraft possible. I felt this would attract attention from the US, and it turned out

I was correct, but for a time many loads went through there. Carlos is doing time to this day in a US prison.

This trip was not the first time I had bellied in an executive twin turboprop. Some years earlier, I had flown a nice 8-passenger high-wing twin from Truckee airport to Oakland airport. The airplane belonged to Val, one of the Old Smugglers who needed to get to a meeting and his regular pilot was not available. We took off and flew to Oakland without incident. When I entered the pattern and turned for final, I activated the landing gear. It felt like it deployed but I did not get three green lights on the dash. I requested a low field pass so the Tower could verify my gear. They said it looked down and locked. I landed without incident then once parked at the FBO (Fixed Base Operator), asked their resident AP (mechanic) to check the gear circuit. On our return, he told us he had located the problem, saying we were good to go.

We took off and raised the gear without a problem. When we arrived at Truckee airport, I tried to lower the gear without success. This aircraft had accumulators instead of a manual crank for a backup due to the high wing configuration and its corresponding difficulty connecting manual linkage to the landing gear located in the wings. Accumulators are air tanks that are pressurized by bleed air from the engines. When activated, the pistons under pressure force the gear down. With these, you get only one shot and then the tank must be slowly refilled by the engines.

When I activated them, nothing happened. I declared an emergency with Center and proceeded to dump fuel for the next 30 minutes. You don't want to go skidding down a runway sparks flying with two wings full of jet fuel. As I went, I purposely flew through localized thunderheads hoping the turbulence would drop the gear. It didn't work.

When I finally lined up on Reno's long military runway, I noticed all the emergency trucks were at the beginning of the runway, not halfway down where I would actually end up. I guess they didn't want to risk me tumbling into them as a fireball. They also had not foamed the runway.

I gently lowered the plane down on its belly. We skidded a little distance, causing a shower of sparks, and came to a rest. There was some small amount of smoke in the cabin from the carpets that heated up to melting point. We evacuated to the runway and were greeted with the sight of all the fire trucks racing towards us with lights and sirens. As I walked, I picked up a piece of belly skin which sits on my desk to this day.

My contract flying days were short-lived, as the business was being increasingly dominated by Colombian cartels who killed competition, literally! I stopped flying drugs and went to flying cash for Thomas, one of the old smugglers who had an ongoing operation in Canada. I would load a small plane full of cash, then fly to an uncontrolled airport (no tower) on the Canadian side. I would spiral down as if to land but would execute a "Touch and Go," which entailed landing but immediately powering up to take off again. This maneuver is used by students to practice. It made it appear that I had landed. Once airborne again, with my transponder now switched off, I would fly low and slow through the mountains across the US border. Radar was not effective in these mountains due to the terrain. It was also generally set to alert only above a certain speed so they didn't get false signals from birds. Once across, I would fly to another uncontrolled airport, do a touch and go gaining altitude like an aircraft that just took off, turn on my transponder, then lose myself in with all the other small private aircraft to fly to my destination.

Another favorite method was to fly low and slow over a road winding through the mountains across the border. If the radar operators did see me, I looked like a tall semi-truck so did not elicit a response.

Through and during all these various endeavors, I made sure my wife was safe and had anything she needed. We traveled the world diving all over the South Pacific, Caribbean, Indonesia, South China Sea, and many others. I took her sailing with friends all over the Caribbean. We visited Paris, took a barge through the Champagne region to the Cote d'Azur, played in London, Venice, Monaco, Hong Kong, Bali, Macau, Tokyo, all over Italy, and the rest of Europe. I built a couple dance studios for her until she decided she wanted to go to college for a degree. We were living in Lake Tahoe at that time so I sold the house I had built for us then moved us down to San Luis Obispo where she enrolled at Cal Poly.

We lived in a nice house, stayed in 5-star hotels,

but there was always the awareness in the back of our minds that we could not let our guard down lest we slip. I was constantly in the air or on the road in dangerous places always with high stakes. Lots of cash and drugs and ruthless people. This wore on me, and it must have affected her. She had to try to have a normal life, have normal friends, always making up stories to explain how we lived. I was always telling her that I would quit as soon as we had enough even after I resurfaced.

For my part, I had to juggle identities keeping track of who and where I was at a given time. I had to spot problems and problem people before they could cause catastrophe. I would come home wrung out not wanting to be social then leave again. I knew she was drifting away when I lost the engine in my plane at night. I had no choice but to put it down in a muddy field hoping it wasn't a building with its lights off. This was not the first time I had an "unscheduled landing," but it was the first time the press got wind of it. Other incidents I would tell her about once I got home or not at all. This time I called her, knowing it was being reported, to tell her I was OK. She was indifferent, saying yes she had heard with little emotion.

CHAPTER 9

FLYING

In my late teens, I flew right-hand seat with friends in their airplanes, so I picked up the basics. As my various businesses grew, I recognized the benefit that having my own airplane would afford me. I had flown by myself without a license for years. Finally, I felt I should get one to avoid potential discovery. Because of my previous experience, I aced the solo flight and test to gain my license. This Private Pilot's license I considered more of a learner's permit since you are allowed to fly only under Visual Flight Rules. This means you cannot land at airports where the weather, or other causes, limit visibility to distances "under minimums." You are also not allowed to fly above 18,000 feet. Many aircraft have higher serviceable ceilings than this. These aircraft, if Turbo Charged, Turbine powered, or Jet powered, operate much more efficiently (read faster with less fuel) at higher altitudes.

I would keep a fast single-engine airplane which allowed me to be most places I needed to be within 45 minutes. When I picked up one of these, some years earlier back east, I was on the way home and came up to a squall line over the Rocky Mountains that was higher than 18,000 feet. While I was picking my way through the Thunderheads in the dark, lightning traveled between two clouds using my plane as a conduit. This knocked out my radios and navigation equipment. I dead reckoned to Salt Lake City where I had to be "Light Gunned" in. This would come up later in a DEA investigation. When they asked who owned the airplane, I told them "a flying club that I was a member of." They then tried to trip me up by asking, "if it's not your plane why was it you who picked it up." I answered that I was the only one qualified to fly it. It is important to anticipate any possible question so you can have a ready response when going in to be interviewed. Not the kind of traceable trail I wanted to leave.

Once home, I titled the plane as a flying club. To complete the picture, I put ads in a number of small airports with phone number tags people could tear off. I didn't actually take any members, of course, this was just to allow me to stay anonymous in case. Unfortunately, the incident in Salt Lake City connected me to it. I kept my modes of transportation secret so that they could be used as corroborative evidence supporting testimony given by customers who had been busted. For this reason, few of my customers knew where I lived or that I flew in, just that I was less than an hour away. I would buy older nondescript American cars to leave them at various airports so that I didn't leave a trail renting. Also, so that if a house I visited was under surveillance, they would A) not know who I was, the cars being registered to fake names at drop boxes, and B) that they would not think me high enough on the food chain to arrest and alert the subject of their surveillance that he was hot.

This did come into play on one occasion that I know of. Geno, a guy I had known for years, who was a regular customer, was popped, and it came out that he had been under surveillance for months. During this time, I had visited more than once. The police went rounding up people who had been seen, and I simply never went back to that car. They described me in the affidavit as an unknown male.

Geno would eventually roll and try to set me up to get out of his 5-year sentence. After 2 years and too soon for him to be out, I got a call from him. He was at a local restaurant and wanted to talk. I went to meet him but knew this was likely a setup. When I walked up to his table, he introduced me to his "girlfriend." From her eyes and demeanor, I immediately recognized her as a Cop. I deduced they had offered him a "get-out-of-jail-free card" if he would help them set me up. This was after I had surfaced again, and they were trying hard to collar me. We went outside to talk, and he immediately started saying incriminating things. I was sure he was wired, so I told him I had no idea what he was talking about and walked away. He disappeared once again, no doubt back in serving the remainder of his sentence.

In time, because I was flying so often at night, in poor weather, and over mountain ranges, I had a number of "incidents." This convinced me I needed a twin-engine aircraft. Understand that not all twin-engine aircraft can maintain altitude on only one running engine. In fact, in flying more than most things, you walk a fine line between efficiency and safety. For this reason, many high-performance light twins are so hard to control if one engine is lost in particular configurations that no one could ever react quickly enough to avoid a crash. I purchased one of these, which was also one of two models of airplane that were considered the fastest Piston-Powered light twins made. This particular airplane was a prototype, a one-of-a-kind unit. It had large cargo doors which did not allow for pressurization; however, without the weight of that equipment and structure, it was a real hot rod. It had been sold originally to the Israeli military who used it to fly weapons to South Africa among other missions. After shuttling it back to the US through Greenland, the broker sold it to me. Now I needed to qualify for a multi-engine rating and retest for instruments since to fly multi-engine aircraft under Instrument Flight Rules I needed a multi IFR rating.

I could not log the vast majority of my flight time for obvious reasons. So when I met with the FAA inspector at Clearlake to take the test, he thought I was a novice. I flight prepped the aging Beechcraft Travel Air I had rented for the test because of its docile flight manners. We took off, and immediately the cockpit began to fill with smoke. I declared an emergency then began looking for a place to put down through the small side window that I could open to see out. I went through the emergency procedures and landed on a dirt road. The inspector and I were jumping off the wings while the plane was still rolling, fearing a fuel explosion.

It turned out to be some wiring that had been added with new radios arcing across some too close insulation.

Surprisingly, the inspector was willing to return to give me the complete test a couple of weekends later. This time we took off without incident, and the inspector proceeded to put me through the test. When we got to the simulated engine-out emergency, the inspector had me put on a hood that allowed me to see the dash but nothing outside. He then placed his notebook in my line of sight, hiding all controls and instruments. He pulled one engine so that I would have to gain control of the aircraft, figure out which engine was out, and configure the plane for level single-engine flight. I was then expected to restart the engine.

I accomplished this quickly without problem except that when I tried to restart the engine, it would not come back online. Now we had a genuine engine-out emergency. I declared an emergency, identified the nearest suitable airport, and executed an engine-out landing. The inspector told me he was not able to put me through the entire test, but he was not getting back on that airplane, so he signed me off as passed. I left the airplane there to be retrieved by its owner.

I flew my airplane extensively for years, finally selling it to Jono's brother. I replaced it with a similar, newer model that I bought from one of my former customers who had been busted and needed to pay legal bills. This airplane was much more comfortable and only slightly slower. It was also pressurized, so I and my passengers did not have to wear an oxygen mask at altitude. It served quite well to shuttle bankers or potential buyers to various projects. It also was very convenient when my wife and her friends wanted to attend a show in Vegas or when we vacationed in Cabo or the Caribbean.

I finally, regretfully, sold my plane to reduce overhead (and visibility) while going legal.

Throughout my time in the business, I was

careful not to do all the things that got people convicted, like talking on the phone or calling from home. I left no paper trail and would not talk in front of a stranger. In fact, if a customer had a stranger there when I walked in, I would leave and never contact him again. If someone called me with a deal too good to be true, I knew that this is how they get people to make an exception to their rules. Greed is a powerful lure and must be controlled. It makes you do things or allow things that you should not. Law enforcement counts on this.

In addition to that mentioned above, I devised various methods for delivering or picking up designed to prevent detectives from putting together enough to get a warrant or a conviction. I would require my customers to have a garage I could pull into and close so an observer could not say they saw me take something out or put something into my car. This was because of the difficulty in gaining a conviction solely on the testimony of a co-conspirator. There must be some corroborative evidence. I would park a car at a public location, hide the key, and then call from far away to tell them where it was. No one could testify they received anything from me. I always wore gloves so no fingerprints, etc. I would drive in ways designed to trip up a tail. I would never break my own rules, no matter how tempting the deal. Finally, I would not run any program indefinitely. Many times I stopped a program even when everything was running smoothly. Usually because I felt, after going over scenarios in my head, that they could have gotten wind of it and be following up the chain. On at least one occasion, I almost quit too late with Law Enforcement only just missing me. It is impossible to know if there were others since I would have to be caught to find out. I wasn't.

The Spider Gear smuggle was different in that I did not end it. I arrived in Lima, Peru, on another routine trip carrying a load of cash. By this time, I didn't need the false-sided briefcase because the people Lalo was working with were well connected. I would arrive and be escorted past customs directly to a car by the driver who would deliver me to Lalo's compound. I say compound because even in the wealthiest of neighborhoods, your house was surrounded by a 10-foot concrete wall with broken bottles stuck on top. Peru had a rebel insurgency going on for years, and it was not uncommon for armed men to break into houses to take hostages for ransom. They especially liked foreign businessmen.

When I arrived, Lalo informed me that their contact had been arrested, so they could not send another shipment. Now I had the problem of getting the money back into the States. It is illegal to bring $10,000 or more into the US without declaring it. Coming from Lima, my known history made flying to the US not a good option. I booked a flight to Mexico City then put $10,000 bundles of cash in individual envelopes and spread them throughout my luggage in suit pockets, shoes, shaving kit… places like these. It was a lot of cash.

When I landed in Mexico City, I had my best relaxed, this-is-no-big-deal face on. Remember, I had been through Mexico City from Lima dozens of times. The one time I was searched was when I was creating a diversion. In Mexico City. On previous trips the inspectors wore uniforms. This time, the inspectors looked harder, wearing business suits with sunglasses. Not sure what was going on, but this inspector told me to open my bag. Once opened, he began feeling through the clothing. He came up with one of the envelopes. He asked what it was. I casually responded, "money." He asked how much. I told him unconcerned, "$10,000." He continued feeling around, finding two more. Same question. Same answer. By now, I figured at worst he would take some of the cash. To my surprise, he put every envelope back into my bags and waved me through. I don't know if my relaxed demeanor made him think I must have heavy connections or what, but whatever it was, he wanted no part of it. I called Jono, who had come with me to India before. He met me at the Tijuana airport in his GMC Jimmy. We threw my bags in back, removed the cash, and stuffed it behind the rear speakers. Then we picked up a couple cases of Tequila to give us a reason for being down there if asked. We were both very experienced, so expected no problems.

We finally pulled up to the inspection booth. The agent greeted us and asked how long we had been in Mexico. Jono was driving, as it was his truck, and he said, not thinking, "just for the day." The agent looked back at my luggage then sent us to Secondary. I had been there before, so I knew that one practice was to let travelers sent in sit for a while to make them nervous while being watched on cameras.

I decided that sitting there waiting was what someone trying to smuggle would do. So I jumped out and walked up to the thick glass window, knocked on it, and said, "not sure if you know we are out here to be inspected." A heavy-set older agent came out. As we walked back to the truck, I was thinking to myself, "wait for it." Sure as hell, the agent says with a matter of fact tone, "so what are you smuggling today?" I responded without hesitation in the same tone, "we're just making a booze run." He barely looked at the truck then released us to go.

CHAPTER 10

TRUST ME BROTHER

I had all along been buying, improving, and selling real estate. Because I had decided to go underground, I could not expand or earn a track record with lenders. Once I decided enough time had passed, I began buying and developing property in LLCs (Limited Liability Companies) with stock owned by me in my real name. LLCs are issued EIN#'s (Employer Identification Numbers), which are their Social Security numbers, so my Social Security number was not the focus and didn't ring bells. Until I got farther down the road and had to file my own returns. I had also been promising my wife I would quit for years. I realized it was only a matter of time before she would be over it and me. Little did I know.

While trying to make connections with legitimate people in the real estate development business, I was able to learn how things were organized. This allowed me to begin to figure out how I might work the angles. I linked up with Eric, an attorney who I met buying and selling properties over the years. He had all the trappings of a successful dealer and was generous with many of them, loaning me vintage race cars and sailboats along with giving me access to clubs and groups I would not have had otherwise. Eventually, I mentioned I had some cash that I needed to get into the real world (read launder). Eric was all too happy to accept a portion with the promise of showing me how to acquire foreclosed properties from banks for pennies on the dollar with little invested on paper. Sounded like a good way to put myself on the map with banks so I agreed. Months later, after learning and watching him buy a number of these properties, I inquired when and how they would end up in my possession since I understood that they would be sold to me by the bank and were not. After a number of evasive and unconvincing explanations, I confronted Eric in the driveway of his sizable mansion. His flippant answer finally was "What are you going to do, sue me? Good luck." He obviously had underestimated the "street" in me. After jacking him up against his garage door, I calmly explained to him that I would not sue him; he would not be around long enough for that. He signed the properties over to me. It is counterintuitive, but I found that people in illegal business were far more honest and trustworthy than those in legal business. This, I believe, is because the illegal people have no recourse but violence should there be a dispute. To be sure, there were disputes, but the penalties and risks taken daily by these people made personal disputes seem of lesser import. For this reason, the parties involved were much more agreeable. I also believe that the criminals who reached a certain level had to get their ego under control in order not to ruffle or bring unwanted jealousy from others who could make waves. In short, the criminals had to be more mature.

When I was illegal, people would routinely hand me millions of dollars in currency or product without the slightest hesitation. They did this even when they had no idea of my real name or where I lived. All they had was the person with whom they had an ongoing business relationship's word that I was trustworthy. Surprisingly, very few people at this level ever got ripped off.

On the legal side, you had to count the number of fingers you got back after shaking hands with some people. These people hide behind the law, always trying to take advantage no matter how.

After getting possession of the properties, I had to do a crash course on real estate development and construction or lose my investment. This is because all these properties had hard money loans against them. Hard money is money loaned based upon equity alone without concern for the borrower's credit history. These loans typically were made at far higher interest rates plus added upfront fees to offset the increased risk. I developed a good relationship with the lender company on one of the properties (a family-owned business). This relationship would continue through many properties over a number of years. I managed to see a return on my investment after much hard work with a few lucky breaks.

Now I began running scenarios to identify the best route forward. I figured out that I needed to reduce my costs so I could sell for less. I had realized that every percentage point the effective purchase price is lowered, the number of people who can now qualify for purchase financing relative to their income goes up exponentially. This can be accomplished by lowering the actual sales price or by lowering the interest rate on their purchase loan. Both reduce the buyer's payment, so lower the monthly cost, which means more can qualify relative to income. Conventional banks have lower interest rates but also have strict allowable debt-to-income percentages. Most people are not aware that a developer who wishes to sell quickly by increasing the buyer pool can "pay down" the interest rate for loans offered on a particular project. Typically, the developer will pay a sum sufficient to offset the interest decrease for 6 months to a few years so the interest the buyer sees is less by that amount for that period.

It is a bit intimidating applying for an institutional loan (conventional) under any conditions. For someone who had never done so, it could seem daunting. Especially if that person had been living outside of the system for the majority of his adult life, so had avoided any kind of paper trail. I began applying with one institution after another, get their rejection explanation, make adjustments, then reapply to another. Eventually, I would find a bank that would approve the loan. In this way, I learned much about banking and banks. Soon I was taking down properties repossessed by the bank, some 100% financed by the bank. I would even sometimes get the bank to loan me the cash to make the payments. I preferred small boutique banks whose officers could act quickly. Some would also offer an unsecured business line of credit as an incentive to bring your accounts under their roof. At one time, I could call my banker and have him deposit over $1,000,000 in my account to use as I wanted. The downside was it lulled me into a false sense of security.

Now able to make all-cash offers on properties, I could buy for less so could sell for less. Then once developed, I would increase the number of buyers who could qualify for a loan by paying down the interest rate on pre-packaged loans I would offer on my projects.

I still needed extra income so cast around for some program that did not involve smuggling. Around that time, a friend who had been both a customer and a source at varying times contacted me to let me know he was getting out of the business. He offered to put me together with one of his contacts. This contact, Larry, was in San Diego. Apparently, he had an excellent connection for large quantities of coke. Larry would have no market with my friend retiring. He lucked into his connection somehow, convincing the connection that he was an experienced mover. I was concerned that this fit the script used by law enforcement to trap someone like myself. I had a face-to-face with the friend offering this connection. After a few subtle tests designed to expose a setup, I was comfortable this was not a police operation.

When I met Larry, I immediately could tell he was presenting a front but not to cover being a cop. Any undercover would have been far more polished. Instead, it was instantly apparent to me that Larry had little if any experience at this level. Once again, I found myself trying to educate an inexperienced neophyte on the dangers and methods to avoid them while working in this business. Needing the source, I accepted the risk believing my experience could keep me out of trouble.

The first time I went to pick up inventory, Larry directed me to a vacation rental near Lake Arrowhead. I arrived on time, and Larry escorted me to a bedroom that had kilos of coke stacked to the ceiling. Despite the risk of losing everything now that I was surfacing and owning property, I began moving weight supplied through him.

I would send an employee to Texas, driving a truck with a camper, to pick up supply. I built a couple of innocuous, identical American used cars with an easily accessed compartment so Larry could simply park nearby, walk to the other car, and be on his way with loads of cash. I even flew into various remote, uncontrolled airports to meet his supplier, who also flew in, so we could not be tracked. During this time, I required that Larry stop selling smaller amounts. This is a problem because it is closer to the street, selling to end-user civilians who are easily tracked and caught. They could then be used to climb the ladder to higher-ups. I could tell that he had no street sense, so would not see things that should ring alarm bells.

At the same time, I had a side business of financing other people's special (read illegal) projects. I had periodically taken investors on some of my own, so now started sourcing money for others. I had never lost any money invested before, so had standing offers from a few friends that if I thought a project had a good chance of success, they would invest. I had friends approach me regularly looking for seed money, so after checking the plans for various "projects," I would broker the money needed. Typical return was 3 to 4 times your investment in a very short time, usually a week to not more than a month. I would charge 25%, so if $500,000 was invested, the return to my people would be $1,500,000 (at 3x), and I would be paid $125,000 with no risk.

After one successful smuggle, I was paid in new $500K blocks of sequential $100 bills. Not sure where these guys got them, but I was happy to pass them along to the investors, opting instead to take the dirty used money for my fee. You never know who or where these blocks were acquired, but you can be sure there was a record somewhere. The last thing I wanted was to be connected in this manner to a stranger about whom I knew nothing.

CHAPTER 11

WALK AWAY

Eventually, I came to a point where I was no longer willing to take the risk of living outside the law. I had spent my entire adult life to that point immersed in this world. The toll on me was becoming unbearable. I was always on alert, as though any moment I would have to act to survive, because I did have to act quickly so many times. Every little breach was blown all out of proportion. I spent fully half my waking time running scenarios in my head to make sure I didn't miss anything, then worrying way out of proportion for small things I was unable to neutralize. In short, it was no longer romantic or exciting; instead, I had PTSD just as though I had been living in a battle zone. Because, of course, I had.

I told everyone I was out, then I put Larry together with Geno and Stan, my two largest customers. I wished them all good luck and walked away. A few months later, Stan contacted me. I went out and reconnected with him on a secure phone. He told me that he had completed a few smooth buys through Larry. This time, however, when Geno was supposed to go down again to re-up, Larry had contacted him to change the meeting place to a hotel room at the last minute. He asked what I thought. I told him it was a bust, don't go! Worse, I found out later that this was a larger than normal buy because Stan had been offered a significant price reduction if he could up the quantity. Classic set-up procedure. He allowed his greed to overrule his sense, and my opinion, then went down to be arrested. I postulated that Larry, with me no longer keeping a hand on the reins, tried to develop a new market without knowing how and was arrested. Once arrested, he was flipped and gave up not only Stan but, I found out later, also me. They wanted Stan but also wanted to get him to testify against me. This was, as already mentioned previously, because of the difficulty in gaining a conviction solely on the testimony of co-conspirators. There needs to be some kind of evidence or overt act like $1 million in cash flown to San Diego.

They ran into a problem, however. Stan, who they got, refused to testify. He was sentenced to 12 years during which the DEA would revisit him, offering to shorten his sentence or even release him if he would help them with evidence to get me. Each time he would get word to me that they were trying again. A stand-up guy! Stan completed his full term before being released.

In addition to Stan, there was Geno who I had also introduced to Larry. He was also busted around the same time! I do not know the details but feel certain that even if he was not also set up, he was identified for investigation by Larry. Geno, I had known going all the way back to the orphanage. He is the one I already mentioned who tried to entrap me.

I continued working on my Real Estate business while also traveling to the Middle East and Hong Kong for special banking, to the South Pacific for diving, and a dozen other hobbies and/or enterprises.

All the while, I continued beating the bush for a new way to support Jenna's and my lifestyle.

My wife and I were living in San Luis Obispo. She was in school, working on her degree, and I was out doing business most of the time. I was finding out how expensive it was to get out of the business. I was supporting two lives, one legal and the other not. Paying taxes on larger declared incomes that now needed to be explained because they were being spent, declared, taxed, and identified as to source. Not to mention that I needed to sever all connection with previous years by moving, etc. In addition, it was very risky to have illegal income since if I was caught they could take everything I had as fruit from the tainted tree.

Add to this, law enforcement would periodically attempt to trap me. I would get a call from an acquaintance who would ask my help in a purchase or would be notified by a friendly banker that my accounts were being audited. I would try to renew my passport and have it take over a year despite my many inquiries. People would try to befriend me in my regular bar then ask me to get them something. Recently when I moved to a new small town, I was approached by the Chief of Police from a neighboring town who made me aware that the Chief of my new town was a friend of his. This was totally unprovoked and he then gave me his card saying to "remember him"? Many others were less obvious but were listed in the documents I got through the Freedom of Information act. I spotted every one so was acutely aware of how much they wanted to catch me up. Still, I managed to keep a good sense of humor even when I got a random call from the Contractors State License Board saying they had received information I was involved in illegal activities. They threatened to pull my license until I pointed out I had not been even charged with a crime.

I needed to always be on the hunt for explainable income. So when flying in and out of my home airport I kept noticing a beautiful piece of land that had roads and pads on it but was apparently not being used. I checked the County records and got the owner's name. When I contacted them wanting to buy, they told me they had owned it so long that the recapture of taxes, etc., would be prohibitive. I asked if there was another property they wanted, which there was. I suggested I buy that property and do a 1031 tax-deferred exchange with them. They agreed and I obtained close to 1000 acres of prime subdivision land. This project would demand more of my time but would keep me closer to home and my wife. It also would require significant investment so I continued looking for ways to fund without smuggling.

As I was juggling with all of these different lives trying not to go crazy without warning, Larry shows up at my house. He had been busted, as I mentioned previously (and set up my other customers) only slightly more than a year earlier. Now he told me a story about having been at the low security side of Lompoc Penitentiary working maintaining the local golf course when he decided to walk away. I could not believe this was the best story they could come up with. There is no way a guy busted for the quantity he was would get a low-security posting even with his cooperation. I again refused to acknowledge anything he said and sent him on his way with my best wishes. Years later, I suspiciously "ran into" him again in my local bar. He told me he could have put me away if he had testified. What he did not know was that I had requested and received my FBI records under the Freedom of Information Act. They were heavily redacted but there was mention that I was known to drive one of the cars that I had earlier modified to have secret compartments. The only person who knew about those was Larry. My answer was "You set

Geno up and you tried your best to put me away but couldn't." He loudly protested that he had not rolled until I mentioned the car. I have not seen him since. After Jenna graduated from Cal Poly, I sold our current house for below market to a banker who had become a friend. Kind of a reward for his helping me purchase a number of properties. Some of these were behind in loan payments to his bank and he would give me advance notice so I could make an offer to the bank before anyone else. He also provided me info on loan amounts, etc.

I then purchased an unfinished house in Marin north of San Francisco. I finished it up and we moved in. Jenna got a good corporate job in her chosen field. Almost immediately, I felt the climate between us change.

CHAPTER 12

HOW CAN I MISS YOU IF YOU WON'T GO AWAY

My wife's corporate job paid her a good salary; still, I never asked for her to chip in. I restored a beautiful little classic Mercedes, which I gave her for no occasion, believing gifts mean more if given when one is not expected. Despite an outwardly idyllic life, I was noticing she was not very engaged with me. Laying in bed one night, I told her I could tell she was not happy. She said little. I mentioned that she had never lived on her own, having moved from her parents' house to mine. I told her I thought every person should live on their own for a period of time to get to know themselves better (I had some experience in this area). I then suggested she might move into her own apartment so she could be free to figure out where she wanted her life to go. I was genuinely concerned with her happiness, even if it meant giving her up. I went on to say I would, of course, pay for everything. To my surprise, she jumped at this with totally unexpected enthusiasm. Before I knew it, she was settled in an apartment in the City. Wishing to give her breathing room, I never asked where her apt was, and she never invited me.

By this point, I was feeling very discarded and not appreciated. I told her I would go to therapy with her if she would find someone she was comfortable with and make an appointment. She did this, so we went. Within the first 20 minutes, it was obvious to me that this person was there to ease me out, not save our marriage, and I said so. Some days later, I invited Jenna to my house for dinner, which I cooked. We were sitting, with me feeling like I didn't know the person I had loved and cared for for so long. She sat, seeming unbothered by any negative emotion or even empathy for the guy who had given her his loyal, unquestioning love for years.

Finally, I said, "Do you see us ever getting back together?" She answered, "I can't say that" (whatever that meant). I thought about this for a moment, then said, "I want a divorce." I did all the legal filings, drafted a Marriage Settlement Agreement, then petitioned the Court for the Dissolution of our marriage, without an attorney. The Judge said it appears all is in order, so she granted my motion.

Jenna and I had minimal contact after until the law who had been copied on the public record knocked on her door. The agents told her she should help them build a case against me. Next, they threatened to take the alimony I was paying her if she did not help them. She declined! I guess she did care for me a little or felt guilty. Whatever the reason, every time I have had contact with her since, she has apologized to me? Not sure why. Our contact has been limited to maybe a dozen times in the last 30+ years.

I believe I know who I am and understand myself more than most as a result of my experience being an orphan growing up alone. This helped me to start over, suddenly trying to figure where I wanted to go. Still, it was neither easy nor clear.

I found there was one silver lining to this devastating experience. As I was at home feeling a great sense of loss and overwhelming dread at the prospect of going out to meet and date, there was a knock on my door. When I opened it, standing there was Tiffany, my wife's best friend, and the person she brought along on our first date. I had always felt she was the most beautiful, sexy, and intimidating woman I had ever met. I invited her in. Within a couple of minutes, she had me on the floor, clothing off, and inside her. We dated on and off for a couple of years, then trailed off.

Now single but not wishing to get back into the business that had supported me for so long, I still needed some extra income. My Real Estate development and construction business was profitable but required I put everything back into the next project.

I continued with various other projects in areas that interested me but, more importantly, had the potential for income. One such project was my brief stint as a music producer. I have zero musical ability myself, but I do appreciate good music from a wide variety of genres. As it happened, Jeff from the Vintage clothing store had invested in a recording studio. When it was struggling and in danger of losing its lease, I had spotted him a few months' rent to carry the studio through. Unable to pay me back, he instead gave me a block of time in his studio that I could use or sell. Around that time, I had a friend, James, who was, I thought, a good blues guitar man, so I got him into the studio and we produced a CD. Not finding a market in the States, we turned to Europe where it was well received. To promote it, we booked James into the summer series of festivals and fairs all over western Europe. He and I had a great time that summer with performances from Spain to the Montreux Jazz Festival on the banks of Lake Geneva. It was not my first time at this festival, but it was the most memorable. We went on to hit small and larger venues through Freiburg, Germany, to the Rock House in Salzburg, Austria, then to Lake Como, Italy. Not profitable but well worth it.

Next, I turned a hobby into a business. Having educated myself on the workings of gas turbine and jet engines for my earlier profession, I now looked into them as a possible income opportunity. I filled out the forms to qualify to bid on "lots" of engines being liquidated by the U.S. military. Surprisingly, I was approved.

I was aware that in order to be always prepared, our armed forces keep spare engines in inventory in case of conflict. It would not do to have to order spares if war broke out, so they had to have them on the shelf. When the aircraft or tank or other item that used these engines was replaced by newer or more able units, the spares held for the now mothballed units would be sold at auction. These auctions sold "lots" consisting of from a dozen to as many as fifty engines. I would bid on the lots I wanted and if won, would take a few of the engines I wanted and sell the rest. I would get as many as possible in running condition and over time became the go-to guy for hobbyists, schools, and all manner of tinkerers all over the world. By the time I shut it down, because of dwindling supply, I was selling in 15 countries and all over the U.S. My engines went into drag boats, offshore racers, as backup for manned gliders, and as teaching aids for trade schools. They were used to de-ice private runways in Canada, were placed in bar stools and raced, were placed in motorcycles, in generators, on hang gliders, and a guy in Switzerland even built a jet pack (not sure if he got off the ground).

Besides exploring new areas for business, I also filled free time with hobbies and adventures. I had been into cars all my life, indulging this interest by buying and selling (sometimes restoring) all types of exotic sports and race cars. I owned and enjoyed many vintage Ferraris, one of which is now worth over $3,000,000. Of course, I sold it many years ago for far less. I purchased a vintage British race car literally in boxes. I then assembled it to the highest standards myself. I drove this car for years, both on the street and track. Eventually, it was becoming impossible to get it cleared for emissions, so I decided to take it on one last trip. I put it in a shipping container bound for England, where I would drive at the Goodwood historic track. Of course, I brought the girlfriend du jour along for fun. After Goodwood, I put the car on a ferry to Normandy, France. We visited Mont Saint Michel, then drove through the countryside to Paris. We drove down past the Arch De Triumph, past the Eiffel Tower to the Left Bank, where we stayed for a few days, enjoying the food and scenery. I had been to Paris a number of times, but my girl had not, so we shopped at the Marché aux Puces (antiques flea market), did the Musée D'orsay, the Louvre, and a dozen others. When we had our fill, we drove down to the Loire Valley to sample wines and stayed at a beautifully restored Chateau. Continuing south, we came upon Carcassonne, a medieval walled city that had avoided destruction in the world wars. We decided to drive in without knowing that vehicles were strictly limited on the narrow ancient streets. To our surprise, the guard waived us through the gates, so we drove up to the 5-star hotel that people waited years to stay in. We found out that a vintage race car tour was ongoing, with this picturesque city being one of the stops. The guard must have thought us part of it. I parked my car among the Gullwing 300SL's and Birdcage Maseratis, then went to the front desk where we were informed that one of the participants had cancelled, so they had a room for us. Sometimes it is better to be lucky than good.

The next day we said goodbye to all our newfound fellow racers and headed south to Barcelona, where we spent a few days touring the buildings of Gaudi and partying until the sun came up with locals on the beach. We never did figure out when they all slept because we would stumble off the beach at dawn to sit at a café to find one of the friends we were with on the beach waiting for us.

After Barcelona, it was through St. Tropez and Nice to Monaco. We stayed at the Hotel de

Paris next to the Casino where I played Baccarat (Bond, James Bond) while my girl got the royal makeover in a spa built inside the solid rock cliff overlooking the harbor hundreds of feet below.

Next, we headed into Italy down the Italian Riviera, past Portofino, to Forti dei Marmi, a resort on the beach which is reputed to be where Italians vacation. We spent our days in our palapa on the beach where every day, the Hermitage Hotel would put out a spread of food on the beach that defies description. We took road trips to Florence to buy leather goods, Milano for high fashion, and Venice for sightseeing. I had been to Venice on my first honeymoon and would later be married, by the mayor, to my second wife there.

We left Italy heading back to visit with some friends who were in Aux de Provence. While there, I was contacted by a guy I had met at Goodwood who was interested in buying my car. We settled on a price so he took the TGV (bullet train) to Nice. I met him at midnight in the train station where he gave me a pile of Euros and drove off. As I walked to the platform to catch the train back to Aux, I heard my name called out. When I turned around, I found a friend from my hometown in Marin. Small world.

Sometime later, I decided I needed to have a yacht so I bought a 65-foot Express Cruiser powered by two 12-cylinder Mann engines, each as big as a mid-sized SUV. I rented a berth in North Beach Miami that was 10 minutes from the airport. In my yacht, it was 4.5 hours across the Gulf Stream to the Bahamas. I serviced it myself, installed an 800-gallon-per-day water maker, a compressor to fill scuba tanks, and a hydraulically lowered swim platform on the stern. Enjoyed having friends down, going on diving trips for a time. Then while riding my road bike up Mt. Tam, back home, I was run over by a construction truck.

I have been an avid bicycle rider since I was in the orphanage. I would ride to the top of Mt. Tam at least every other day (when I was in the country) for over 30 years. Over the years, I had been injured in crashes, but this time was serious. My back was broken in six places. I also suffered cracked ribs, a broken leg, and my shoulder socket was punched through. Most of it healed quickly, but my back was in bad shape. I could barely walk or stand without excruciating pain. Even sitting was almost impossible. I was told there was damage to the nerves coming off my spinal column. Worse, they could not operate until my back stabilized. For the better part of the next year, I was functionally crippled. Finally, I was down on my boat when I got a call from my surgeon to say that they had a new procedure. He felt I was a good candidate so I was on the next plane back. I arrived in the morning. By that afternoon, I was being prepped for surgery. The following morning, I was able to hobble to the bathroom. My doctor advised that he had reattached some nerves that might take months if not years to reconnect. I noticed immediately that some were not hooked up as before because I would try to move one leg and the foot would move. Fortunately, my brain adjusted it out quickly. The biggest challenge was learning how to walk again. All went well and I was back on my bike in no time. Some areas remained numb for years but eventually came around and today I am stronger than ever.

CHAPTER 13

THE WHIRLPOOL

Back at home, I continued subdividing, then building high-end houses, as well as buying, renting out, and selling commercial income properties. I would eventually own properties in a number of cities ranging from Las Vegas, Nevada, to Savannah, Georgia.

The older smugglers I met in the beginning were still working. They had become close friends with whom I spent holidays and recreational trips. Theo had a close call that required he leave the country to avoid arrest. Val retired, and there were a few I lost track of. Thomas, however, had been running a huge smuggle for years, including all the far-reaching logistics required to transport thousands of pounds of Hashish from Pakistan to Canada. Once sold, they would then transport hundreds of millions of dollars in cash to Europe, the US, and Pakistan. People focus on the actual contraband but forget that transportation of this cash is a separate smuggle on its own. Law enforcement is acutely aware of this, so put significant resources in place to seize these profits.

In addition, if one wishes to enjoy or invest these monies without leaving a trail that can be followed to the smuggler, the cash must be introduced into the system without tripping alarms. I had devised ways to accomplish this albeit on a smaller scale for years. The popular method in years past was to simply open a Swiss Bank Account. Switzerland had for hundreds of years positioned itself as a banking haven, passing laws to protect the privacy (read anonymity) of its clients. All one had to do is open a numbered account which was not attached to your name so if asked the banks would cite the law restricting them for providing any information. Everyone from the Nazis to Mob bosses and Despots to Tax Cheats or Jewel Thieves around the world enjoyed this service for years. The US government with others deciding this cannot continue put the arm on Switzerland to open these records. The US controls in large part the international banking system. Any bank barred from access to this system would be almost instantly out of business. Under this threat, the Swiss government and so their banks began providing account information.

Enter the offshore banking industry. Small countries in need of a new source of income after tourism, etc. began to pass laws making them attractive as banking havens. These countries included Caribbean Island countries, Middle Eastern countries with no oil, Central American countries, even Communist countries. All had their own spin on it in an effort to avoid strong-arm tactics of the sort used on the Swiss. Many countries begrudgingly gave in. Some allowed access if asked but also required that all records be destroyed 6 months after an account was closed.

I knew about, and long had used, Hong Kong for laundering cash because of its relationship with the Communist Mainland. You could put cash in a Hong Kong-based Mainland Bank where it was effectively in Communist China then transfer to a western bank and know that the trail ended there. If you were caught smuggling, for example, the police would trace the money that you used to pay for everything from rent to food hoping to find and confiscate your ill-gotten gains. If you had a loan that allowed you to buy your house, law enforcement would attempt to find its source to see if maybe the company who made the loan was not legitimate and instead you had simply loaned your own money to yourself through a shell company. If you had credit cards issued by your employer for expenses they would attempt to show the same and would charge you with money laundering.

When the US tracked cash to having been sourced from a Communist bank or select Middle Eastern countries and demanded its original source, they would hit a brick wall. Unfortunately, this also included the possibility, if contacted, that the Communist or other country might confiscate your account and cash. For this reason, it is important to prevent the investigators from following the trail to the bank that makes the loan or other accommodation. Investigators can try to backtrack, knowing the loan company's name from your title, but they can do nothing if they cannot show that the funds were yours and sourced from illegal proceeds.

In order to ensure this break in the trail, I would open numerous accounts in many different banking havens for multiple shell companies based in the same country as their account was located. Next, I would deposit in one, transfer one to another through multiple banks in different countries. After each transfer, I would quickly close each account. If law enforcement went to the bank where the end funds to buy my house originated, they would ask the source of the funds. The bank would, after some time for research, provide this. Then law enforcement would go to the country where the next company/bank named was located. They would again demand the records which, after some time for research, would be turned over. It would go on like this until inevitably the next company/bank account had been closed more than 6 months so all records had been destroyed. End of Trail.

This is a tedious, time-consuming pain that understandably would be eventually ignored. Corners would be cut allowing law enforcement to document you depositing cash with your passport, game over. Also, with computers becoming always more powerful and faster, the bank-to-bank wire transfer is quite easily located. All that is needed is the final source and the rest can be traced backwards. The only way to break this chain would be to physically take the cash out and carry it to another bank which accomplishes nothing. There were things like bearer bonds that can have large face value and are not attached to any one person. I'm not sure if they even exist any longer. Crypto opens many possibilities but did not exist then. So if a person had large amounts of cash that they wanted to use and spend, the first thing to do is not get caught doing whatever they did to get the cash. This is why I said repeatedly to my friend that he had more than enough why keep taking the risk. Unfortunately, greed, as I said before, is a powerful emotion that is difficult to control so he kept going. Even if a person does stop working before getting hot, they still need to be careful not to spend in any way that would trip alarms or focus attention on them. I had been investigated many times by various agencies over the years. Because of the way I set things up, these investigations always went nowhere.

Thomas and his partners were constantly wrestling with this problem. This got me thinking that there might be a way to earn without smuggling or dealing. Real estate development is profitable but requires expertise to navigate the process and laws. It also takes time to get from raw land to "ready to build" pads, so it requires enough reserves. There needs to be sufficient cash available to pay for the land, property taxes, surveying, multiple studies, then often an Environmental Impact Report. Conventional lenders do not lend on raw land development projects because they have no income to cover the interest payments. Plus, land is harder to liquidate due to a smaller buyer pool. This leaves "hard money" lenders who typically charge very high interest with origination fees, or a Developer can bring in investors through a private offering designed to avoid SEC (Securities & Exchange Commission) regulations. Every development property I purchase, I put in its own stand-alone single-purpose LLC. This allows me to bring in partners by issuing stock without changing ownership of record. Important because an applicant obtains "vested rights" at various stages in the process which can be lost with ownership change, depending. It occurred to me that this then could lend itself to investing with a certain degree of anonymity while requiring no day-to-day management. Profits then could be distributed through sales.

This also provides a documented legal source of funds.

I suggested to these guys that perhaps I could solve some of the problems they were having with the tremendous profits they had coming in.

I explained that I could only protect their funds if kept independent from them. If they got lazy and or cut corners by using the accounts set up for these investments for other purposes then law enforcement would find and track the investment.

They would set up accounts in secure countries then deposit cash into them and transfer to a secure end account from which funds could be transferred to a development project's LLC ownership account. This should be the only fund transfer from that account after which it too would be closed. Then, when the development was completed, profits out of sales could be deposited into new accounts which would have no connection to illegal cash. These profits would be paid to the partnership interest which they acquired by sweat equity, commissions for bringing in the deal or any number of other reasons that did not include paying cash in. Tax returns would be filed with payment for taxes due after deducting their share of depreciation or other costs associated with the property.

Now having run all the possible scenarios with their likely outcomes in my head, I realized that human nature being what it is, at some point one of the people involved would cut corners. Someone would fund the development project from an account that they had used for other things and/or fail to close that account after. This then would subject the Development Project to exposure if those involved were ever under investigation. Once found it would not only expose the Development Project to seizure but might expose the person who purchased and managed the Project to a charge of Money Laundering. Money Laundering is a crime which carries a maximum penalty of Life in Prison.

In order to protect myself from this potential outcome, I would need to have good answers to the obvious questions, i.e., "If this is an investment, how did you connect with the investor? Where is the correspondence? And finally, where is the contract that would be expected with such an investment?" This kind of supportive documentation cannot be generated after the transaction is discovered, or it would be easily proved fabricated. Groundwork must be laid at the time the investment is made if it is to survive scrutiny.

Realizing the problem, I placed ads in the London Financial Times and Asian Wall Street Journal seeking investors in any project that was intended for my friends. I then generated correspondence of the type one might expect between the potential overseas investors. This would culminate in a contract or agreement. I would have the investor side translated into the language of their origin, even on one occasion Urdu, the Pakistani national language. Then, I would pay a translator to retranslate so I had a record.

Once complete, I would give the people investing letters to post when they were in the country they work in so that I had canceled stamped envelopes to monument the documentation's origin. This seems like a chore but is preferable to life in prison. In fact, when this group did get busted, I was not charged in a case that was the largest in US history at that time. Thomas and his partner received multiple life sentences for "Money Laundering."

Funds transferred to my accounts from an

overseas account were tracked to my accounts because, as I had anticipated, Thomas's partner had sent them from an account that could be traced to him. Once his huge ongoing smuggle was exposed, my records were subpoenaed and reviewed. After review, I was not charged.

Instead, one afternoon while cooking BBQ for a couple girls, one of which I would later marry in Venice, Italy, on the Bridge of Sighs, there was a knock on the door. When answered, it revealed a DEA agent who served me a summons to appear as a witness for the prosecution. I had my attorney contact the prosecutor to explain that I intended to exercise my constitutional rights against self-incrimination. The court's response was to grant me "Transactional Immunity," which eliminates my right to refuse to testify since I am now immune from prosecution for anything I say on the stand so have no exposure.

I still had no intention of testifying so told them so. The court's response was to declare me a "hostile witness" for the Prosecution. This then created a problem for me. If I do not answer questions, I can be declared in contempt of court and be jailed for up to 18 months or until I agree. What's worse, the contempt of court charge can be renewed after 18 months for an additional 18 months almost indefinitely even after the trial ends. This had happened to a friend some years earlier. If I answer but lie on the stand and this can be proven, I would be subject to the same penalties as the defendants in the case. Nevertheless, testifying against my friend was still not an option I would consider.

I knew that I had been very careful for the entire time I had been involved in illegal business. I did not do anything that could be connected or that could incriminate me beyond a reasonable doubt in criminal activity. I informed my attorney that I intended to try to walk that fine line of testifying without giving evidence against my friend. His response was that in all his years he had never known or even heard of anyone successfully accomplishing this. Once on the stand, I will be on my own and not entitled to confer with an attorney since I am not charged.

When I arrived at the courthouse on the designated date, I was directed to a waiting area. Upon arriving at the end of the hallway, I observed a large room full of those waiting.

There were at least 50 people, many of whom I knew and who had agreed to roll over for a reduced sentence. I figured the likelihood that this room was monitored by cameras was high. My plan to walk that fine line would be in jeopardy if I walked into that room and was observed on camera being familiar with these "Co-Conspirators."

I looked to my left, to a smaller room occupied by a number of men in suits. I would later find out that this was the attorneys' lounge. As I was sporting a very nice Brioni Italian suit, I felt I could blend in, so I entered that room instead to wait for my name to be called.

Once on the stand, I acknowledged knowing Thomas. It would have been pointless to deny since we had been friends for so long. He and his wife had been to my wedding, etc., etc. I described our relationship as diving partners and friends. I denied any knowledge of any illegal activities and then spent the better part of two days explaining real estate investment and development as I was questioned about money wired into various project accounts.

I gave them nothing on him. He was convicted anyway, a victim of dozens of others who did testify against him. It was also difficult to pick an impartial jury from the pool drawn in an area where the median income was less than $50,000 for a trial to include up to a billion dollars. The charge was money laundering. Arguably a victimless, non-violent crime for which he received multiple life sentences. The severity of the sentence, I believe, was a result of his refusal to implicate others in addition to his multiple country fugitive run lasting many years. He was finally captured when he was lured, by a trusted friend, who had been turned, to a country which had an extradition treaty with the U.S..

Money laundering as a crime requires the law show attempts to obscure the true origin of money being introduced into the financial system no matter if from illegal activities or simply to avoid paying taxes due.

When the law requested the bank in Dubai, that was the origin of one of my transfers, to provide records on the source of the funds in question, they "were not forthcoming." This came from an affidavit in a later case being used to attempt to seize cash found in my home (those efforts were unsuccessful and the cash was returned). Another incident also used in that failed attempt was the transfer of some hundreds of thousands of dollars from Hong Kong directly into my accounts in the States. This transfer was a bit of an anomaly as I had gone to Hong Kong to receive an investment and after meeting up with the investor (another smuggler) found that he did not have a secure account from which he could transfer. In order to break the chain of any subsequent investigation connecting him to me, I had him withdraw cash. I then deposited that cash into the Hong Kong branch of Bank of America and transferred to my Bank of America account in the U.S.. Since the Hong Kong B of A is a different company than the U.S. B of A, this transfer popped up for investigation. When questioned about it at the time, I explained that it was an investment in a Project. I went on to explain that since the funds were held in a Mainland China bank, I was unwilling to accept a check, so I had the investor provide cash. Since I had not tried to hide the funds by transferring from myself to myself and had declared the money, I had not committed a crime.

It is a crime to attempt to introduce or move cash in any way designed to hide its origin. If you send cash through the mail, you run afoul of the postmaster general. If, however, a person ships by private company and sends from themselves to themselves, this is not illegal. If discovered, the person simply needs to declare the funds, then pay taxes at the end of the year. Costly but not criminal. This method is not ideal since law enforcement can file a civil case against the money itself, which requires the money to show it is not from illegal activities (guilty until proven innocent). This tactic was tried unsuccessfully on me a few years later.

Unfortunately, not being charged with a crime did not preclude the law from visiting the lenders on all of my projects. After implying crimes not in evidence, and for which I was never charged, I saw my loans and credit lines being called one after another. I was effectively put out of business in short order. With little effort, they wiped out the years of hard work I had done to get out of the business to go legal.

As a result, if the commercial buildings and shopping centers I owned all over the United States experienced vacancies, I couldn't offer tenant improvements to lure new businesses or ultimately cover the shortfall between income and amounts due. When forced to sell in order to pay off loans you can no longer service, due to vacancies, you watch any equity that has been earned or invested vaporize. In short order, I was back to scrambling. I was trying to survive all by myself surrounded by people looking to catch me up. I had to dust off the "do or die" mindset that had served in the past.

CHAPTER 14

FIXER

Over the years in "the business," I had met and worked with various "families" all over Europe. Most in the general public are not aware that many of the larger and midsized towns across Europe each have their own independent Crime Families. These families are involved in all manner of illegal enterprises, sometimes cooperating with each other but always jealously defending their territory. In my dealings with some of them, I had gained a certain amount of respect and a reputation as a person who could get things done with a minimum of unwanted attention. Because of this, I had been, on occasion, offered odd jobs by some of these families. Most of these "jobs" were to courier or facilitate the transfer of one or another item of value to a destination, be it a bank, customer, or another family. In the course of this occasional employment, I had been trusted with items and/or cash in significant quantities and value. While working in this capacity, a couple of unexpected incidents also showed I would not give up what I was trusted with. Consequently, I found myself being offered increasingly sensitive jobs.

I have always tried to avoid situations that could require violence, believing this to be the last refuge for a poorly planned operation or a weak mind. That said, I do recognize that any illegal endeavor has, by its nature, the potential for violence because many of the people one is dealing with do not share my philosophy. For this reason and others, anyone in my line of work must recognize that violence may be necessary, so they must be willing to act. While the killing of another should be a last resort reserved for the worst of situations, it must be kept in the toolbox.

Keeping all of this in mind but finding myself in need of cash, I, for a time, began accepting jobs that were not limited to the delivery of money or items such as gold and diamonds. Some of these jobs would put me in considerable danger but did pay handsomely and in cash.

For example, the following is a job that I did shortly before retiring from this line of employment:

I was contacted by a Family I had done work for previously, whose territory was a port town in the south of France. It was explained to me that this Family had agreed to cooperate with another Family based in a town in northern France to pull off a job in Antwerp, Belgium. They did not tell me the nature of this job, but as Antwerp is a major hub for the Diamond industry, this was the likely target. Apparently, upon the successful completion of this job, the Family in the north did not feel they received all that they were due, so they grabbed the courier from the southern Family when he showed up to deliver their share. The person grabbed was not just any soldier but was in fact one of the many children of the boss of the southern Family. The northern family was demanding a sizeable ransom for his release. Now, before I go on, it bears mentioning that this "kid" was, in fact, a grown man in his 20s who was neither a nice nor attractive character. I would describe him as an arrogant thug. Nevertheless, the job I was being offered was to somehow return him to his loving (snic) Family unharmed.

To be sure, the southern Family, which was much larger and more powerful than the Family from the north, had at their disposal an army of "soldiers" willing to carry out all sorts of mayhem if ordered to do so. This army, however, was more of a blunt object than a precision scalpel. If released, it could cause irreparable damage, bring unwanted attention from the authorities, and/or result in harm to the hostage. On the other hand, the southern Family could not simply pay, as this would damage their already tarnished reputation and could open them up to similar acts in the future. What they needed was someone who could enter hostile, well-guarded territory, unseen, free the hostage, then return him unharmed. For this, they were willing to pay and provide logistical support. Make no mistake, if I was caught, I could expect no help from them. In fact, the kid would not be intentionally harmed, at least not right away, because he has value. I, on the other hand, could expect swift retribution of the most severe kind.

I ran a few scenarios in my head and then contacted the Family with a list of things I would require to take this job. They, in anticipation of my request, had already managed to insert a young woman into the home town of the northern Family. She was able to find the location where the kid was being held along with other useful intel without being discovered. She met me at the airport in London with the keys to the untraceable car I had asked for, in addition to a trunk full of other gear. I asked her to lunch, then spent another hour picking her brain for useful tidbits she had collected but did not place enough importance on to include in the summary that she gave me with the keys.

Once done, we bid au revoir and parted ways. The reason I needed to get this "lay of the land" is that crime Families place great value on information, so employ an army of taxi drivers, housekeeping staff, waiters, even police who all report any unusual person or event happening within that Family's territory. It is for this reason that the Blunt Object approach was a non-starter; for any soldiers from the south entering the town up north would be quickly recognized and dealt with.

I now had to infiltrate this town. Knowing that an American entering a moderate-size town in northern France would be quickly reported (my French was a bit rusty), I chose to "hide in plain sight." I checked into a modest hotel under a company account, wearing a cheap suit, then spread blueprints all over the room for any prying eyes. I left promptly at 8 am and did not return until after 5 pm to further paint the picture I wished to be reported. I had also, on my way, stopped at a sexual toy store to pick up a few items. Handcuffs are not something you want to explain to security at the airport. Fortunately, they are readily available the world over at any sex shop; I chose the pink fuzzy ones. I also picked up some ball gags.

Now established, I needed to verify my intel, so I found the same little park across from the apartment building the girl told me about. I sat on a bench appearing to listen to music with headphones, staying until the late afternoon. I found all to be as described, including her detailed description of the structure of the building.

The next day, I found and purchased one dark blue baseball cap with a white short-sleeve shirt. This was the uniform worn by employees of a fast-food delivery service which the girl had mentioned after my prompts during our lunch. I had before arriving studied the routes in and out of the area to familiarize myself sufficiently to be able to follow any of them from memory. Now I drove all of them to verify the maps and to see if there were any closures or work being done. Ready, I parked the car around a corner then walked to the apartment building entrance wearing the cap and shirt. I carried all my gear in a brown paper bag inside a semi-transparent plastic bag like those I had observed the delivery people carrying. I entered and took the elevator to the top floor. I located the access door for the roof, jimmied the lock, then once in disabled the mechanism so that it could not be opened with a key. Once on the roof, I laid out and prepared my gear, after which I settled in where I could see the car that the men watching my subject used. This position also allowed a view of the area immediately in front of the entry doors. At slightly before 7 pm, I observed a man walk to the car, get into it, and drive off. Based upon the girl's observations, there were likely two men watching the hostage, so now he had only one minder.

I quickly ran to a spot directly above the apartment where we had concluded he was being held. I grabbed my ropes and went off the edge of the roof to lower myself down to the balcony on the kid's side.

This building was of a very common mid-century modern design, built, I am guessing, between the 1940s and 1960s. The standard floor plan was of a common living area consisting of a kitchen and living room flanked on either side by a single bedroom. A balcony running the entire length was accessed by sliding glass doors. Because the bedroom to the right, looking from the street, had lights on and off regularly, we had guessed this side to be for the guards, leaving the other with no lights for the hostage, hopefully. The building had fifteen floors, with the apartment we were interested in on the seventh.

Once hanging at the correct balcony, I hooked my legs over the rail and landed. I immediately slipped the rope from its attachment on the roof, dropping it quietly behind bushes below. It would not do for the returning minder to notice ropes hanging from the roof past the hostage's balcony. I then went to the sliding glass door to jimmy it open but found it unlocked. Pushing the drapes aside with my finger to my lips for silence, I found the kid laying on the bed looking at me. My gesture was not needed as he had figured out why I was there the minute he noticed me silhouetted on the drapes by a streetlight across the way. Now he pointed to his leg and something I had not anticipated.

Most of these 1950s and earlier apartment buildings in Europe were heated by central boiler systems, providing steam to radiators in the individual units. His captors had chained him by the leg to one of these radiators so that he could reach the bathroom but not the door. I removed his handcuffs easily, but when I inspected the lock on his ankle, I realized this was a high-end lock which would be very hard to pick. I had not thought to bring a bolt cutter but always carried a set of picks, so I set to work on the lock. It took much longer than I had budgeted for, but finally it clicked open.

Quickly motioning for the kid to make a noise to get his captor to investigate, I put my rope gloves back on, then positioned myself behind where the door would swing. One knocked-over chest later, the door opened. In stepped a guy seemingly as wide as he was tall. I tagged him with a closed fist to the back of the head, and he dropped. In my experience, better than half the time this blow drops them, but if it doesn't, it also knocks out their eyes temporarily, so there is time for a second. I use a gloved fist because using a bar or other tool risks grave damage or death where a fist generally will not. I was not there to kill for reasons already stated but also because these families are very tight, so if you kill or maim one, the rest will hunt you until they exact revenge. The last thing I need is a bunch of crazy French Gypsies chasing me back to the states looking for revenge.

I handcuffed and gagged him, then relieved him of his gun, money, and phone. By this time, cellphones were becoming more common so had been embraced by career criminals tired of carrying rolls of quarters for pay phones. We quickly positioned for the return of the remaining guard. We needed this guy to step far enough into the room for me to get around the door behind him. We also needed him to be facing away from where I was hiding. I positioned the kid to one side out of sight with instructions to get the guy's attention once he was in. Because I had taken too long picking the lock, we barely had time before we heard a key in the door.

This guy was taller. He came in, bag in one arm, with keys in the other hand. Once in position, his attention on the now free kid, I tagged him. This guy did not fall but stumbled forward a couple of steps. The kid, who was his height, caught him mid-stumble. He went down hard, so I handcuffed and gagged him while the kid relieved him of his weapon, cash, and phone. As I turned to leave, the kid gave this guy a couple of vicious kicks to the ribs. I later learned that this one had treated the kid rather poorly while in captivity. I think the kid would have happily kicked him to death had I not stopped him. I was anxious to get on the road, thinking that we might have as much as the entire night before someone found these guys and raised the alarm. My hopes were quickly doused when the second guy's phone began to ring in the kid's pocket.

Neither of us had any intention of answering it, but this created a serious problem for us because when no one answered, whoever was on the other end would likely come to investigate why. This meant that instead of hours to get out of hostile territory, we probably had only minutes. Once in the car, I had the kid lay down in the back seat so we did not appear to be two. I then decided to take the least likely route to safety: a long trip north through Switzerland, Austria, and Slovenia to Trieste, Italy, where I knew another crime family that was friendly and who also was on good terms with my employer.

This was a route I was familiar with from my earlier European tour promoting the CD I had produced. It would take around 6 hours, but I was confident our pursuers would not think it likely as our escape route. It seemed I was correct as the next 4 hours passed without a problem. It was early morning, still dark. We had made good time approaching the Slovenian border. Slovenia, I knew, had pretty much an open border on this local road. We crossed without incident, but almost immediately we passed a rest stop where I noticed a larger Mercedes enter far behind us. As we had been alone on the road for some time at this hour, it caught my eye. We were driving at a good speed, but the Mercedes began trying to catch up to us. I turned off to a road I had traveled previously, knowing it to be a winding, less direct route. The Mercedes followed. Slovenia is a country that was once part of the larger Soviet Union. Since independence, it had developed its own organized crime syndicate known to have fingers in everything. They were also known to be exceedingly violent.

The Mercedes kept trying to close the gap which I, having had experience ditching the police back home, worked to maintain. After a number of frustrating failed calls, I managed to contact my employer, on the phone he had provided, to report our location and apparent situation. I then concentrated on my driving, winding towards Italy. By the time we were approaching the Italian border, I had managed to put at most a mile between us. Now, however, we were going to have to slow to get through the little town before the border. It would not do to be pulled over carrying firearms, especially with a guy whose last name was well known in this area. Approaching the crossing with no sign yet of the Mercedes, I noticed two cars on either side of the otherwise deserted road. From their exhaust in the cold predawn mountain air, they were both idling. More troubling, they were both facing towards the road I was on. I maintained my speed until the last minute, then floored it past them, hoping to catch them off guard. To my surprise, they made no effort to stop us. Instead, in my rearview mirror, both cars pulled in, blocking the road behind us. These were, I realized, sent by my employer to block our pursuers who I could now see in the distance approaching quickly. I did not stick around to see how it ended up.

Recognizing that our car was no longer anonymous, allowing those wishing to do harm to locate us, I felt it prudent to drop the Kid with the friendly family so they could see to his safe return. Once the job I had been hired for was in this way complete, my attention turned to my own safety. I drove directly to the Nice airport, parked the car in long term, then caught a flight to London. From there to New York and then home. My employers, to show their satisfaction, had my pay plus a 10% bonus deposited to the account I had opened for this job.

CHAPTER 15

JUST A POOR FARMER TRYING TO SCRAPE A LIVING FROM THE LAND

I was now divorced, so I had no restrictions to my sources of income. In addition to conventional (read legal) and unconventional (mentioned above) routes, I explored the California weed market. Marijuana was not, at that time, legal in California. I did have some contacts up north in the growing areas, so I looked at where I might fit in. I turned my wine cellar into a grow room, did make some money, but quickly realized that the established growers had the market mostly tied up. I looked at developing a market back east but found that the big growers already had markets there as well. Then I noticed there was one area in need of improvement: transportation. I kept hearing how these big growers would lose one out of every three shipments sent, to the army of law enforcement all along the way. Especially heavy losses were being seen at the Nebraska and Colorado pinch points. These were the two routes that connected to the interstate through the Rocky Mountains, so funneled traffic and traffickers.

In many ways, this resembled smuggling across borders, which I had years of experience in. I could not afford an airplane, so I set up a transportation system by land using trusted long-haul truckers carrying legitimate cargo. To be sure there were a number of hurdles that needed to be overcome if this was to provide my customers a secure service. Long-haul trucking is strictly regulated and inspected in this country. Trucks have transponders which transmit info on location, destination, and cargo. There are thousands of "weigh stations" located on all major routes where the trucks are inspected for everything from overloaded cargo, contraband, even human cargo. The truckers are required to keep log books which are checked for current licensing, tax payment plus the number of hours they drive between breaks.

Trucks are inspected at these stations for mechanical condition as well so all of those items must be in order. The methods used vary from physical to canine to electronic including X-ray, heat, and even electronic sniffers. Supporting these stations are armies of highway patrol agents roaming the interstates randomly pulling trucks over for inspection. Once being inspected the truck's cargo manifest will be compared to actual cargo as well as previous inspections along the route. We would be transporting weight into the tons potentially so had to create a packing system able to survive. Convincing my drivers to participate required their confidence in my system. Having years earlier received my General Contractor's license I requested a "Bid Set" of plans for the new truck stop to be built on interstate 80 heading to Nevada. This gave me the state of the art equipment my guys were likely to see en route.

Knowing that the sense of smell relies on tiny airborne droplets which are constantly coming off most people, animals, plants, and products, I began designing my containers. I wanted to have the shipper deliver the product to me by blind drop. A blind drop is a way for two parties to transfer a product without having to personally see or have contact with each other. In its simplest form, a truck is parked with the key hidden on it so once away the shipper could safely call to tell where it can be picked up. The party picking up will then approach looking out for surveillance, may electronically sweep for tracking devices then once in the vehicle may drive in a way designed to make any surveillance expose itself. The cargo will not be visible, and there will be no fingerprints on it so even if the driver is stopped it cannot be shown they were aware of the crime. There may also be an ad placed for drivers so if asked the driver can show how they got involved.

This presented me with a problem. The shippers, who were large established growers, lived in very sparsely populated areas. Most were located in or near a few small towns in the "emerald triangle" in northern California. These areas are well known to law enforcement who would patrol or set up random stops on the few roads in and out. Weed is bulky and pungent, so any sizeable quantity is difficult to transport safely. To deal with this, I would provide growers with any transportation vehicle that would normally be traveling these routes for legitimate reasons. These included specially constructed propane delivery trucks, septic pumping trucks, heavy equipment delivery trailers painted to look like known equipment rental companies, or any others one can think of.

Then, when cash was returned, although more compact, it must be run through the same gauntlet. Many of these growers preferred to bury cash in plastic containers on their property rather than try to enter it into the legal banking system.

I recognized this as another area of potential profit, so I set to thinking of a method that would be repeatable, would attract no unwanted attention, and that I could utilize whenever I needed to. I already had a heavy equipment trailer to haul my equipment from job to job. This one had hydraulics to lift the bed at one end so the equipment could be more easily loaded or driven on. I fabricated from heavy gauge sheet steel what appeared to be a fuel transfer tank that fit under the trailer bed in between the frame rails. This fuel transfer tank was split horizontally at a center flange, which also was where the tank sat on the frame rails. Bolts then went through the flange and frame rails, securing the tank and seal. I rigged the top half with an attachment point where a chain could be attached to the raised bed enabling me to ratchet the top half up once unbolted at the flange. The top was heavy enough that even a number of men would have difficulty raising it. Inside was a space large enough for several million dollars. On the top, I attached an access panel which if removed revealed a space which appeared to be as deep as the tank. This space gave the appearance of access to the interior of the tank but was in fact a steel pipe of a diameter larger than the access panel so its blacked out sides were invisible. I would fill it with diesel fuel so in the unlikely event that it was inspected all would seem normal. The filler pipe which went sideways to the outside rail of the trailer was attached to this center pipe so if measured it seemed to go to the bottom of the tank. This installation with its fuel load added to the weight of the top.

With the top of the tank raised, money would be deposited. Then the top would be lowered to sit on a rubber gasket between the two halves at the flange. The bolts would be threaded in and torqued. The tanks would then be pressure washed to prevent dogs from alerting. Many people are not aware that money in large quantities can trigger dogs, since much of our currency is in close proximity to drugs at one point or another, so it picks up droplets. Also, at times, I would drop money and pick up more weed. To complete the picture, I would put a commercial piece of equipment on the trailer, ostensibly to be delivered to a job or local ranch.

Many times, I would come around a corner on one of the winding roads to find a police stop with dogs and people out of their cars handcuffed.

Once I had the product, I would vacuum-seal it in plastic, throw it into my swimming pool, then move it to another area (to limit contamination) where I would double bag and vacuum seal again. It would be washed again and placed in a specially constructed crate that looked normal outside. Inside the crate was glued and sealed with construction adhesive so if the screws were removed, it still could not be opened. Next, sheet metal would be placed in the interior, left floating loose. Inside this was placed special heavy plastic used to wrap buildings against weather. This plastic readily adheres to itself with a heat gun so it creates a hermetic container. The Product is placed in this container with a bag of activated charcoal, which absorbs odor, then sealed within by heat gun. The space between the sealed plastic container and the free-floating sheet metal would be filled with sand. The sand's job was twofold. It would add weight so the crate was not light for its size, a sign of a fluffy organic cargo which officers look for. The second reason was sand's natural ability to scatter and block x-rays. If x-rayed, it is also suspicious if the x-rays are blocked completely so the multiple layers of sheet metal, sand, and sometimes lead pellets, glued in a pattern on the sheet metal, give a picture of cargo without allowing today's sophisticated x-ray machines to highlight organic matter. X-ray equipment back in the day simply sent Gamma Rays through a container or luggage. Because different materials would scatter the rays to varying degrees, a shadow picture would emerge. I had long ago learned how to fool these using everything from lead (which blocks) to bananas which naturally emit low levels of gamma rays. For this reason, industry had developed x-ray equipment which used computers with different sensors to read the backscatter then paint a picture in color highlighting organic matter, which' includes drugs and other contraband.

Finally, the crate is labeled, palletized, and sprayed with clear urethane. Clear urethane seals any tiny particles that might be on the crate to the surface so they cannot become airborne and picked up by dogs or sniffers. The crate is banded or wrapped again with the shrink plastic. If anyone tried to drill into it, the drill would hit the sheet metal. Because it is free-floating backed by sand, the drill will just push it in without penetrating.

I was able to package 250 lb crates quickly, so from delivery to me to my blind drop at the other end was only 2-5 days depending on when I had a truck leaving. I charged by the pound so didn't have to grow or sell. Because I required my pay be in the vehicle left for me at the destination, in cash before I would take it to pick up the crate, I was always paid. I never lost one shipment despite reportedly being scanned by dogs. By the time I shut down, I was transporting thousands of pounds every week. I even heard that after I shut down the operation, Chicago went dry for a week until another group filled the gap.

This is not to say there were not bumps in the road. I worked mostly with three groups. One based in Saint Louis handled states all the way to Arizona, one based in Chicago, and one that handled New York down to North Carolina. None were trouble-free. On one shipment to the New York area, I was to deliver one thousand pounds to a single individual. The van left for me had a cracked windshield which could get me pulled over, so I had to wait a day for a replacement. In dealing with this guy using tosser phones, I found it necessary to tell him over and over not to say incriminating things on the phone. Because of this and other things, I determined this guy was over his head, so should not be elevated to this kind of weight. I decided to give him only half. I put the other 500lbs in a storage facility across from a police station. When I was back in California, I explained why to the client in person. He was happy with my decision.

A month later, the client who had sent the 1000lb contacted me. He requested I pick up what his guy had left plus the 500lbs I had stored. Apparently, the guy I had delivered to was selling by the ounce locally and taking too long. Arriving in the area immediately, I noticed the police pulling people over in the middle of the day to search them. This told me that they likely knew there was a load in town and were hoping to get lucky. So we were hot. I arranged to pick up the remainder of what I had delivered. A very dangerous mission because I had to meet the guy personally knowing that the police were looking for anything unusual and he might be compromised but not know it. When I met him, it was worse than I had imagined. He was a rank amateur trying to look mobbed up. I doubt if he had ever done more than indulge before this. Now I had to collect it, prepare it for transport across the country, then transport it. Making matters worse, I found that the client had told this guy my first name as well as my hometown. My name is distinctive enough and my town small enough that law enforcement could identify me (computers had become so powerful and interconnected that research that used to take days or weeks now was almost instantaneous).

Considering this, I knew I had to get out of the area fast without leaving tracks. To make matters worse, a monster storm was hours away. When I picked up at his house, he told me to follow him so he could lead me safely out of town. At the end of the block, he turned right, I turned left. I drove to the storage where I left the other crate, then built another for the remainder with the materials I had left for crating earlier, before going to pick up. The unit I rented when I delivered, a month earlier, could be driven into and the door closed behind. When finished, I parked the van that had been provided not knowing who it was attached to or if that person was hot. I caught a bus to Newark, New Jersey, where I rented an SUV under an LLC I had created for this purpose. Mobile once again, I drove back and picked up the crates. Then I purposely drove into the worst blizzard the east had seen for many years. Heading west into the storm, the conditions were bordering on "white out" with blowing snow & ice. Soon the only vehicles out with me were emergency vehicles. The road was littered with blown over tractor-trailer rigs. Stopping only for fuel, new tosser phones, and food, I drove straight through. During one stop, I contacted the other group I had been delivering for in Chicago to see if they could take and liquidate this product. I was concerned that some smart cop would figure out who I was then publish a notice to locate the SUV I had rented. These notices also go out to the various agricultural stops at the state lines between my present position and California. There were none that I couldn't go around between New York and Chicago, but there were still troopers out. The Chicago people instructed me to rendezvous in a small suburb to Chicago that I had delivered to previously. They said their man would be at the McDonald's at 6 pm. I didn't like this because in small towns, the local police often frequent this kind of business, but I was in no position to argue.

When I arrived on time, their man was not there, but two police officers were. I was driving a large SUV with out-of-state plates. I bought food, then left. I contacted the people and was assured he would be there in an hour. Again, not there, but a different police car was. I drove slowly by, then drove to the neighborhood I delivered before. This happened two more times, one of which again had the local police there. It is now getting to be late night. I have to assume the police have taken note of me. I am hiding out in the neighborhoods, knowing that the police will not risk a confrontation in a residential area. Most police departments identify areas on the roads in and out of town where they can safely stop dangerous vehicles. They practice the procedure in order to limit the danger to themselves or the community. I considered ditching the crates but felt the police would search for them and find them if I did. Now it was midnight. As I drove towards the house I had delivered to before, finally coming in the opposite direction, I recognized the guy. I followed him to the house. We quickly put the crates in the garage and closed it so I could get away before the police might pass by (looking for me).

I then headed out of town towards the highway. On a straight portion of road, a police car pulled in front of me with another paralleling me to the left and one pulling in behind. They then all slowed to a stop, forcing me to do the same. They had me exit the vehicle, searched me, and handcuffed my hands behind my back. I was then told to sit on the curb. Understand, it is winter at night in Illinois. The temperature was subzero with the wind chill. I asked a number of times why I was being detained with no response. A number of cars roared away and returned over an elapsed time of about an hour. Finally, a detective approached me. He demanded, "Where are the crates?" They had begun treating me as a suspect immediately after they ran my ID. Earlier, when I was killing time driving around the neighborhoods, I had noticed garbage trucks working their routes, emptying dumpsters, so I answered, "Is that what this is all about, me throwing empty crates in a dumpster?" I got no answer. Finally, I said I was getting hypothermic and needed to find a hotel. They asked me what I was doing there, and I told them I was in the area giving a lecture. Now I was looking for an old friend who used to live around here to sleep on his couch but couldn't find the house I remembered. The phone number I had for him was no longer in service, so finally I gave up. They asked his name. I declined to give it, saying I did not wish to cause him problems.

I asked if I was under arrest. When they said no, I said, "then I am going to find a warm bed." When the Detective finally gave me back my ID, he told me, "Don't ever come back to Chicago." I had been told this before in Florida; I didn't obey that time either. I dropped my rental and flew home without incident the next day.

On another trip for this same group, I arrived in Tennessee to rent a full-size SUV to carry the crates to a popular tourist town in North Carolina. I was there to drop product, then after, pick up cash payment from a group I had delivered to before in St. Louis. This was a service I also offered, understanding the difficulty of transporting large amounts of cash safely around the country. I called the delivery phone the night before to be sure all was on schedule. The guy sounded relaxed, said all would be ready for me at 9 am the next morning. I would sometimes try to call when not expected just to catch anything going on unexpectedly. This time, I called before 9 am the next morning to get the location of the drop van. The phone was picked up but no one answered. I could only hear radio in the background. This is not what you want to hear. It means that they are likely in the middle of being busted. This would make sense if they were being surveilled. Law enforcement would be aware that a shipment was incoming because people always say too much on the phone. The police would want to be ready to bust the incoming load and its courier so would bust the group early so they could roll them. The police would then change the delivery at the last moment citing some made-up issue knowing that the courier would not want to return with the product so would likely take a chance. They would do this so that the bust would go down in an area that they had secured and wired with sound/video. Few people in the business would recognize this as a sign of a bust. Most would allow the last-minute change.

At this point, I am in a very bad position. I had

transferred from my trucker's rig to the rented SUV before driving in. This because the transfer from a big rig required I use a standard transfer location arranged for in advance. Normally, at this location because there were no transfer stations I could arrange to use, I would transfer to a rented SUV then use a multi-story or underground parking garage at a mall or hotel to transfer from the SUV to the Van provided. Now I am in an isolated area with only a few ways in and out making it simple to set up checks to trap me. I have to assume law enforcement knows I am within the net. The tosser phone used is anonymous, having been purchased at a convenience store hours earlier, but these can still be traced, once they have the number, by triangulation from the cells that carry the signal. Even if I disable the phone, I am still in the net so can be caught at a check. I could dump the crates and leave fairly safely. They might find them but would not be able to connect me to them even if they could identify me. Dumping or transferring the crates always carries some risk being a suspect activity that might be observed especially with their size. I also did not want to lose the load, ruining my perfect record. I needed to keep the police from closing the net so I could slip out. I gave it some thought, devising a plan. I then pulled the battery out of the phone (cell phones constantly shake hands with cells even when not on a call). I drove to the largest hotel in the area. I went into the lobby, found the restroom, reinserted the battery initializing the phone so it connects with a cell then I dropped it into the bottom of the towel dispenser. It has a better chance of not being discovered there than in the trash which gets emptied more often. The thinking here is that if I am correct about this being a bust, the police will see the phone at this location so assume I have checked in to stay. Again if I am correct they will not want to spook me so will not have checks all over wanting everything to look normal until I remake contact. Triangulation of cell towers will get them a location but is not precise enough to find the actual phone. This requires special equipment with which they could search on site. They will not want to do that for fear of me seeing them. All very speculative.

I figure I have at most 12 hours before the battery runs out or they get impatient enough to go in and locate the phone. Of course, if I have read all this correctly, by that time I will be many states away. I hit the road.

I am not safe yet. Remember, this group compromised my identity in New York, so once the police figure out I am gone, they will issue an alert. I need to get rid of the product fast. As soon as I was out of North Carolina, I picked up another tosser. Figuring my St. Louis clients, from whom I was scheduled to pick up money after North Carolina, might be able to take the delivery, I called them. Thankfully, they agreed to take the product.

Everything went smoothly in Saint Louis. I picked up over $500K in cash. I would never put cash in my trucks for transport, too tempting for the drivers. This I would transport in various ways, including personally by renting a car and secreting it in its structure (I am a better than fair mechanic). This trip, unfortunately, was different because I had to assume there was an alert out on me. If there was, they would likely be able to figure out the vehicle I had rented. I called a friend who had an airplane and arranged for him to meet me at an executive airport in Colorado. This was as far as I felt I could get before entering one of the two northern choke points on the main routes across the nation. I dropped off the SUV by dropping the keys in the overnight box so they would not be processed, and reported, right away. My friend landed on time, so I was safely away. Once back in the Bay Area, after delivering the cash, I called home to check in with my girlfriend, who was watching my dogs. She told me the local police had come by saying that they received a silent alarm; she knew I had no alarm on my house. They asked specifically if I was home. My fast-thinking girlfriend told them I had gone out for pizza. Would probably pass them when they left. It seemed my fears about the police connecting the dots were well placed.

I was always honest with anyone I was in a relationship with. It was only fair, plus it allowed them to be prepared should something go awry. Worked this time with this girlfriend and would again soon; she came through like an old pro.

Some months later, the Saint Louis group was busted. It came out they had been under surveillance for months. The authorities proceeded to round everyone up. One by one, all of their associates were rolled over with one exception. They could not put together a case against me because of my standard practices, so they decided to raid my house before pulling the trigger on everyone else. The thinking, I believe, was to hit me without warning so catch me with something illegal. Or, in the alternative, pressure/trick me into cooperating. What they did not anticipate, even though they could have by reading my historical jacket, was that I would spot the signs, be ahead of them.

Home from my last trip before the Saint Louis busts, I had a pressing problem. I had seen a number of signs that they were closing in on me. These included seemingly innocent calls from the fire department asking to visit my property to verify I had cleared brush before fire season (I knew most of the local firemen and they knew I kept my property clear), Small aircraft flying too low over my house (my house was on a 400ft private driveway and was not visible from anywhere) despite the fact that I am a multi-engine instrument pilot familiar with the FAR's limiting such flights. Finally, of course, the visit to my house by local police saying they got a silent alarm when I had no alarm system.

Before leaving on my last trip, I had taken delivery of some weight. Now expecting a raid, I had to get it away to a safe storage until the owners could pick it up. This was long past the days when I had plenty of alternate ID's. My girlfriend was aware of my past exploits but not that I had started up again. Not knowing how long I had before the expected raid, I crammed 500 lbs of weed into my SUV and left immediately. I needed a place to store it. All that was keeping prying eyes out at present were some blankets.

I called my girlfriend to ask if I could drop by her house. That's all I said but she was so sharp she read my tone. When I arrived she was ready to go even not knowing what the problem was. She wiggled into my SUV sitting on pounds of weed. We found a storage locker of the right size that she could rent just until I could get the product back to its owners.

It took a few weeks but got it done. The raid came a month later. It included Homeland Security, ICE (Immigration / customs), FBI, DEA, Local Major Crimes Taskforce, Local Police, Local Sheriff, and the Highway Patrol. The CIA was the only one missing. Who knows they too might have been there.

My Girlfriend and I were in bed. This was the house I had built a dozen years earlier. It could only be described as a "Mansion." At 7:00 am, I heard a loud banging with someone yelling. I immediately recognized it as the long-overdue raid. I jumped to my feet, ran naked down the hall to the top of the stairs directly across from the front door, in time to see the swat team bust in.

I froze, my gentleman's sausage hanging out, put my hands up and said, "please don't shoot my dogs they will not bite you." My dogs weighed 175 and 201 pounds. My girlfriend, also naked, was struggling to hold them behind me. She would later mention how hot her face felt. I informed her the reason might be all the laser sights that the police had trained on her head, only half joking.

Officers took my dogs and locked them in a room that had an outside door. I neglected to mention that the female knew how to open doors. Within minutes, she was downstairs looking for my girlfriend and me. Felt like a Three Stooges movie.

We were given clothes from my closet then escorted to seats out by the pool still handcuffed. I asked to see the warrant but was told they didn't have to show me one. During the next 6-7 hours, that saw even more police arrive along with forensic teams, the detectives tried to put us at ease so we would talk. The DEA agent guy was the same one I had slipped past years earlier coming back from Atlanta then again after when the IRS called me in.

I had given my girlfriend a quick idea of what to expect months earlier. The detectives did not disappoint. They separated us so they could work on her, thinking she was the weakest link. They were very wrong, getting nothing from her. They used the same old lines I had heard for years, and which I warned my girlfriend they would use. She later recounted that they were word for word what I had told her to expect. I continued to ask to see a warrant to no avail. At one point, a detective came over with great emphasis and said he came all the way out from New York for this. I suppose he expected me to be so impressed that they had tried to catch me on my retrieval trip to New York that I would fold, blubbering, "You got me, officer, there is no way I could outsmart you," then tell all. Instead, I said, "Oh, cool. How do you like it in California?" totally innocently. Next up was my old friend, the DEA guy. He comes over and says, "I have to ask, do you want to cooperate with us?" I told him I would think about it, to which he said, "That's what I thought." He left.

The rest would have been funny if they didn't do so much damage in between taking pictures of themselves in this magnificent mansion. One greasy, sawed-off task force guy kept saying, "We are going to seize all of this." I said nothing, thinking to myself, "This is their best and brightest"? Frustrated by my silence, he said, "I would have shot your dogs," to which I responded, "That's because you're an asshole."

That guy's boss, wearing an obvious fake beard and glasses, kept coming over to us trying to seem nonchalant. At one point, he said of my girlfriend, "She's a little young for you, isn't she?" (mid-20s) to which I answered without hesitation, "Some people are young when they are old and some are old when they are young." Overloaded his brain, I suppose, because he had no response. Finally, I was bored, so I decided to have a little fun. This guy was obviously doing a lot of undercover work, hence the covered face. Any undercover officer's first fear is that they will be recognized, so every time he ambled over, I would say things like, "You look really familiar, have we met?" or "I can't get over how familiar you look." He stopped coming by.

Finally, they transported me to the jail where I was told not to take off my shoes; I wouldn't be staying. My girlfriend had found and called my attorney who had arranged for me to be released immediately.

They were not able to seize the house, had to return the cash they found, and my computer (had nothing on it anyway). Even got my hunting rifles back.

Not the most intimidating raid I had ever experienced.

Some years earlier, a good friend had experienced a similar raid. On a Friday, I get a call from Carl who sold weed. He was away on the East Coast when the law had just that day raided his house. It is not uncommon for the various agencies to conduct these raids on Friday afternoon, expecting that those arrested would be more cooperative after spending the entire weekend in a cell. This expectation is borne of the difficulty of arranging bail late on Friday, as well as judges' habit of leaving early on Fridays.

They serve a search warrant to Carl's wife, Stephane, at their house Friday afternoon. After finding some evidence, they arrest

Stephane to cart her off to jail. Carl wants for his wife to avoid a weekend in jail. Unfortunately, he is far away, plus now wanted, so not able to arrange payment for a bondsman to spring her late on a Friday. He and his wife had been close friends to me since I was first in this business so many years before. He apologized for asking. I assured him that no apology was needed. I was able to call my banker just before the banks were to close to arrange a cashier's check for the full amount of the bail. I then hurried down to the jail and got her released. I was driving one of the many high-end cars I had owned over the years. Because the call caught me at a social function, there was no time to go home to swap to my pickup truck. The look on the arresting officers' faces when they watched Steph leave the jail to get into my car was the same one I now saw on the faces of those who had raided my home when the jailers told me not to untie my shoes.

CHAPTER 16

FULL CIRCLE

Long ago, as a boy, I was trying to figure out what it was that parents imparted to their children, which, because I was an orphan, I had missed. I concluded that one of these things might be a sense of yourself being a person you can be proud of. This allows a person to go out into the world with head held high. It allows them, in dealing with others, to know what is acceptable (for them). To know where your boundaries are allows you as a person to create long-lasting relationships and connections. Understand, however, that this is a two-edged sword. Parents can just as easily encourage the opposite.

I believe it is also the case that no matter how certain a person is about how they would act if ever in an emergency or dangerous situation, there is only one way to be sure. To know, one must experience firsthand a life-and-death situation. In this way, learn what they are made of through action or inaction, as the case may be.

These revelations took on greater import in my life, dealing as I was in life-and-death situations so often. It became of critical importance that I be able to correctly read people quickly. I needed a "tell" which I could use to reliably recognize those who posed a threat if things went south. This, so I could avoid them or at least make sure they did not know enough to do damage if turned. I also would sometimes feed misinformation, assuming that this would eventually fall into the hands of the law.

Of equally great import was the need to identify people who I could count on with some confidence when they themselves may not be sure.

Over the years, I began to notice some telltale traits that seemed to correspond to just the weaknesses I was concerned about. Just as those who claim to be the most intelligent in the room usually turn out to be the least, it became increasingly apparent to me that those who loudly claimed to know that they would be able to act well if ever they found themselves in a life-or-death situation were in fact the most likely to do the opposite.

The San Francisco Chronicle once commissioned a study for $250,000 in an attempt to understand the mechanism for this. The conclusion was, "Dumb people think they know everything so believe they are smart and Smart people know they don't know everything so think they are dumb."

Having the dubious record of being in many of these situations personally, I felt I was uniquely qualified to spot the personality traits or flaws that might lead to failure. This was of paramount importance because to fail even once would have been my end. What I noticed was that people who do not understand the implications of failing in these situations take them too lightly, so believe them easy to handle, then believe themselves capable. Once confronted with the harsh reality, invariably they lay down to give up, it being so much more than they had expected.

Conversely, those who say they hope they would act well but do not know have thought enough to realize the gravity of these situations.

Those who realize the far-reaching implications are more likely to understand that to fold will guarantee a bad outcome. So long as one has not given up, a good outcome remains possible. An example of this was my earlier incident in Atlanta. It initially appeared that I had no options and was caught. By not just giving up, I was able to recognize, then utilize, every potential advantage, with the final outcome being much better.

I often told a very good friend, who is much younger, when teaching her to play pool, that it is not over until it is over. Many times, when I had dropped most of my balls and she had many still up, she would get discouraged, so stop trying. I would tell her, "You are not dead yet." Now she regularly kicks my ass on the pool table. I don't mean to say the loss of a pool game in any way is comparable to the risks I was taking. I am just making the point that this philosophy can be applied to all aspects of one's life with good results.

When trying to spot those possessed of these weaknesses, I designed subtle tests that would allow me to quickly recognize who I could safely work with. I noticed that liars don't trust others because they know they themselves are not trustworthy, so they expect the same of others. In the same way, people who would give up others to save themselves believe that everyone else would also. To vet these people, I would relate to them one of my close calls. Those who did not believe me out of hand were the ones who did not believe they could, so didn't believe I did. If a person doesn't believe they can, then they can't. The stakes were too high for this.

In fact, the need to choose those you can trust is not limited to just identifying capable albeit untested people. It is also important to be able to recognize those who have already been tested and failed. These are the ones who will have been turned by the law and sent back in to trap you. They will be people that you have worked with, so trust to some degree. For this reason, I needed to be able to see that something had changed.

It was always important to know what kinds of actions were suspect, like changing the meeting place at the last minute. Recognizing subtle changes in a person who was trusted is far more difficult. It is easy enough if a person who is known to have been busted contacts you long before they should be out of jail. When it becomes difficult is when a person was caught that morning then turned immediately. In this case, there is no telltale absence or other suspicious occurrence. They might be wired while trying to get resupplied, just as they normally would have.

I noticed when seeing people who I knew had been busted then had rolled over that they were empty in some way, not as they were before. They might convince others that they had not rolled, but they could not convince themselves, so would never again have the same self-respect as before. This subtle change can be seen if you know what to look for. When those who had chosen this "low road" were released from their "reduced" sentence, they would always seem somehow hollow, missing something. They would try too hard to be as before, but it was obvious that they could not convince themselves, even if they were outwardly successful. To be sure, many never had this sense of self to begin with. For me, it mattered little since once a person understands what to look for, all of these people stand out as ones that you would not want to associate with or trust.

I am not saying that being "rolled" is the only way a person might arrive in this unenviable position. There are many reasons that a person might find themselves at this place besides getting "rolled," and there are just as many different variations of the values upon which they are based. These values range from outright thieves or "Holier Than Thou" Proselytizing Hypocrites to Stand-Up people possessed of strength and pride. They are limited only by the depth of lessons taught or learned by experience. There are then also the narcissists and sociopaths who believe anything they do is ok because no one is as good as they are, but this is a mental defect. The signs are the same in all. Those who miss these signals, or let greed cloud their vision, so ignore them do so to their own peril.

This screening out process is something many, who are unaware of why, do anyway, innately because of the gift or curse their parents imparted to them that is now a part of them. I just had to come at it from a different direction, not having parents that I could look to or ask. I had to learn, on my own, that on this earth there are at least as many flaws and reasons for them as there are different personalities. I then learned that understanding any particular defect could be a useful tool while navigating a dangerous world.

When I had finally reached a point in my life where I felt that I could relax, for a minute, I paused to take inventory. I had traveled the world many times over, had earned and squandered many millions, had pursued even my wildest dreams, educated myself in a great many disparate disciplines, even seen great success in most things I tried. Plus, and perhaps more importantly, I had seen myself through the worst of situations, so had gained confidence with the knowledge of how I act in the heat of battle instinctively. This, I feel, is the true measure of one's core exposed, as it is, without the cloak of posturing or pretense.

My chosen path cost me my wife, and almost my life, many times. It also gave me a sense of self that was missing when I was young. I know, like, and respect the person I made myself into. Those things I always felt I had not learned that everyone else somehow knew are now known to me even if I found many of them not so valuable as I had imagined. I do now have a number of real friends who are to me my family. I am in the second half of my life. Because I stayed in great shape, I am in excellent health. After spending so many years running as though if I stopped my life would be over, I now find myself questioning its worth. For maybe the first time in my life, I am without something I feel motivated to work towards. Certainly, I have no regrets for any of the accomplishments that I felt worthy of chasing. It is just that few if any were as attractive, once reached or obtained, as the idea of them which was the impetus for their pursuit.

People always talk about life being so short. I, in contrast, never concerned myself with it ending, so busy was I at the living of it. I have always experienced reality through the reality of the experience. Perhaps it is for this mindset that my older brother described me as fearless?

I have, for my entire adult life, been unafraid to look at myself in the harsh light of truth and have made a point of owning the result, good or bad. Now I keep coming back to a number of truths that I accepted along the way: I like success, I enjoy accomplishment, I apologize to no one for living well or for anything I have done. Still, the one most important thing I really ever wanted is the only thing I was never able to find for long, if at all. That would be someone to love and be loved by. It sounds corny, but to a boy who was never held or cared for when young, it became the meaning of life. Now, with a large part of my life behind me, this one "wish list item" seems increasingly unlikely. Yes, I have had many girlfriends. I even married two more times. But for all the things I did that were supposed to be impossible, for all the accomplishments that people could not believe and those no one will ever know about, for every day spent trying so hard to be all things to all people, I now question if I may have missed the point. It might be that I somehow came to expect more from life than it could ever be possible for it to be. This would explain why I was always unimpressed with so many things purported to be impressive. Or perhaps one of the things that kids can get from their parents is a tempering of their expectations so that they are grounded as adults.

I believe from personal experience that any person can be capable of more than they might expect. I suppose that a person's confidence in their own worth and abilities, or lack thereof, comes not just from their parents but also from things experienced along their way. Then, in addition, it likely must also be, at least partially, innate. We know babies are born with very distinct pre-wired personality traits which affect the way they receive input from the very beginning.

Whatever the answer, I know for me none of this is written in stone. I did not realize until late in my 20s that many people, when considering a new direction or endeavor, ask themselves "can I" whereas for me the question was always "do I want to." I am not sure how I came to this mindset; I just find this difference to be very telling when trying to understand the directions I chose. It seems that, if I am an example, any person could change simply, as I did, by deciding that from this point on, this is who I am. Once decided, you live as that person until one day you wake up and that is who you are.

Cheers.

AFTERWORD

Every detail and event in this book is true, as it happened. It is, however, not the entire story. Many pursuits, adventures, events, and experiences have been left out. Some because they might be specific enough for the parties involved to be identified. Others represent a period when I was doing work as a "fixer" with people who I had interaction with so would not hesitate to come after me if recognized. It doesn't matter how good one is; any encounter can turn bad without warning. For this reason, pursuit is better avoided if possible. None of these interactions am I ashamed of, and I will probably write another book on them down the road. I did include one example in this book that I felt was at low risk for attempted retribution. I also did not wish to relate so much all at once that it would be difficult for the reader to follow. I experienced it all, but even I still sometimes have trouble keeping it all in context.